Indian Deed dated February 20, 1684

This indenture made in this twentyeth of ... Bacans in the
... Congregatione Curam Cora ... Coloford tatava...
... the right of they ... hand subscribed to this indenture ...
... in the name and behalfe of the proprietors of mattaturko
... Cavan Coco ... Coloford tatava cum ko caza ...
... Curans ... notorumable Curans fishes for ...
... ploundi to hand by us overned, or good securitie for that ...
... proprietors ... Chofe absolut full grantid, having ...
... incorporate of mattaturko their ... ground tons ...
... naming ... as followeth: ... uppon ...
... land and ... to ... river: at ... one of ...

...at our lord one thousand six hundred and eighty two: betwene
...Casukim: wenataconj: wechamunck, wenencaske colourins sachem
...one the one party: and Thomas Rudds and John Stanly the other
...new England the other party Witnesseth that ...in...wiwunss...
...wenataconk wechamunck wenan caske colourins sachems
...and consideration therunto us moving and ford the same
...for the payment before the inseling of this indenture hath
...and sould unto the aforesaid Rudds and Stanly with the ratyf of the...
...strators, asignes and...for ever...
...corne or cattell upon that...thing...
...bounds called by the...been...
...quantum...

[remainder of page illegible]

Indian Deed dated December 2, 1684

[illegible] this [illegible] in the yeare of [illegible]

[illegible]

[illegible] John Goodsworth [illegible]

[illegible] John Wadsworth [illegible]

[illegible]

[illegible] one thousand six hundred and eighty four [illegible]

[illegible] of the other part [illegible]

[illegible] nine pounds in hand [illegible]

[illegible] have by these presents [illegible]

[illegible] and from the [illegible]

[illegible]

PROPRIETORS' RECORDS

OF THE TOWN OF WATERBURY CONNECTICUT

1677–1761

TRANSCRIBED AND EDITED BY

KATHARINE A. PRICHARD

CLEARFIELD

Originally published
Connecticut, 1911

Reprinted for
Clearfield Company, Inc. by
Genealogical Publishing Co., Inc.
Baltimore, Maryland
2002

International Standard Book Number: 0-8063-5141-1

PUBLICATIONS OF THE
MATTATUCK HISTORICAL SOCIETY
VOLUME THE FIRST

PREFACE

In this its first printed book the Mattatuck Historical Society publishes certain ancient documents relating to the early history of the town of Waterbury,—originally known as Mattatuck. A brief reference to the early history will explain the origin of the documents and their relation to one another and thus place them in their proper historical setting.

In October, 1673, a petition signed by twenty-six inhabitants of Farmington was presented to the General Court at Hartford, asking permission to "make a small plantation" at "a place called by the Indians Matitacoocke." The General Court, having been advised by men whom they had sent to "view those lands" that the place was a suitable one at which to begin a new settlement, granted the petition and appointed a committee of five persons "to regulate and order the settling of a plantation at Matitack."

This committee, known afterwards as the "Committee for Mattatuck," or the "Grand Committee," had for its task as Doctor Henry Bronson describes it in his "History of Waterbury," "to make rules for the planters and prescribe the conditions of settlement," to act "as the temporary guardians and the fathers of the plantation, with all the power usually exercised by town authorities . . . in fact to found a town and organize it." In pursuance of this task the committee drew up certain "Articles of Association and Agreement," constituting a basis of membership, that is of proprietorship, in the new settlement. The thirty-nine persons who signed these articles,—thirty-one of them on the 6th of June, 1674,—constituted the organization known as the "Proprietors of Mattatuck," and afterward "of Waterbury."

The original manuscript of the "Articles of Association and Agreement" was doubtless retained by the General Court, but a duplicate of it, in the handwriting of Major John Talcott, the chairman of the committee, is still extant. Having survived the vicissitudes of more than two centuries, it was carefully framed between sheets of glass, and is in possession of the Mattatuck Historical Society.

These Articles constitute, no doubt, the earliest remains of the doings of the Committee for Mattatuck, but are not included in this volume. They are given in Bronson's History, as taken from the copy in the handwriting of John Stanley found in Waterbury Land Records, Volume II. A comparison of this with the photographs of the duplicate, reproduced in one of Miss Sarah J. Prichard's chapters of "The Town and City of Waterbury," will show many inaccuracies in the copy, and the omission of one name.

The other surviving records of the doings of the committee—excepting the letter of April 5, 1682, which appears in the Appendix—constitute Part First of this volume.

At a meeting of the Proprietors in 1711—a quarter of a century after the Grand Committee had ceased to act—Mr. John Southmayd and Deacon Thomas Judd were instructed to "view some writings of the Grand Committee," with the understanding that such as were "of value" were "to be recorded, the remainder to be obliterated," and eleven years later action was again taken with regard to these same or other similar "writings," namely, "that those papers that Deacon John Stanley shall present, setting forth the acts of the Grand Committee relating to the settling of the town, shall be recorded," unless recorded already, "and those that are not deemed needful shall be returned to Deacon Stanley."

What "writings" were "obliterated" we have no means of knowing, but the records which remain to us are evidently incomplete. We have the minutes of less than a dozen meetings between 1677 and 1682, containing such orders and regulations of the Committee in relation to the settlement at Mattatuck as their office of supervision involved, and in some instances confirming the previous action of the planters. We have also several letters of instruction and three lay-outs of land.

The Grand Committee was the centre and source of authority, but as the plantation became well established they sought to relieve themselves of their burden of responsibility. At a meeting held in February, 1680-81, they decided that "for the future the inhabitants of the place being orderly called and convented" shall have liberty to choose their civil officers "without any further order from the committee." In 1685, a majority of their number having died, the General Court authorized the two survivors to "continue their powers as Committee for Mattatuck, but we have here no record of their action later than 1683, except a grant of land in June, 1687, and a letter in September of the same year."

Their task may be considered as having ended when the incorporation of the town took place. An act of incorporation was applied for—"a patent for the con-

firmation of their lands unto the present proprietors"—
in May, 1685, and was granted by the General Court a
year later.

To these "proprietors" the Grand Committee, having purchased the Mattatuck lands from the Indians,
had "assigned and made over all their right and title"
in 1677, "the inhabitants having paid the purchase to
our order," as the committee phrased it. In the
"Articles of Association and Agreement," already re-
ferred to, there is set opposite the name of each subscriber the amount of his subscription, the smallest
being limited to fifty pounds and the largest to one
hundred, but the relation of these subscriptions to
the actual ownership of the territory is nowhere dis-
tinctly indicated. "That there was a purchase of the
township made by the planters in some form," Miss
Prichard remarks in her fifteenth chapter in "The
Town and City of Waterbury," "and quite distinct from
the purchase from the aboriginal inhabitants is evi-
dent, but nothing definite or explanatory concerning it
has been left on our records." She suggests that the
arrangement was similar to that adopted in Massachusetts Bay, where "the proprietors became holden
to the colony, through the committee appointed by it,
for all the costs and charges incident to the settlement
of the plantation." In each case the planter "secured
lands according to his venture in the common stock,"
but in Massachusetts the original allotment was left
to the governor, while in Mattatuck it was left to the
Grand Committee.

The names of the men who became by the action
of the "Committee for Mattatuck" the proprietors of a
territory embracing a hundred and thirty-three square
miles are spread upon the pages of Bronson's History,

and Miss Prichard in her twelfth chapter gives interesting facts concerning them, including personal characteristics.

But the fact that concerns us here is that these Proprietors kept a record of their proceedings which came to be known as the Proprietors' Book, and that a large part of the present volume (Part Second) is occupied with an accurate reproduction, a "verbatim et literatim" copy, of this Proprietors' Book, or at least of what remains of it.

In his History of Waterbury, Doctor Bronson refers to this Proprietors' Book as "an old, dingy manuscript, of foolscap size, which he had dug out of a mass of forgotten rubbish found in a private family." Describing it as it came into his hands he says: "The sheets are sewed through and through, in the middle, by a cord of unnecessary strength, and the whole is covered by coarse brown paper turned over at the edge, with a broad margin, and made fast with a thread. Many leaves are gone at the beginning and end, and those that are left are rent and broken, and exceedingly brittle when handled. Only fifty-four pages remain."

The late Frederick J. Kingsbury, LL.D.,—the first and only president of this Historical Society until the time of his death in 1910,—in a first draft which he had prepared of a preface for this volume, suggested that the "forgotten rubbish" of which Doctor Bronson speaks, "consisted of books and papers, left by his father, Judge Bennett Bronson, who was well known as a student of local history, and who undoubtedly had the manuscript in his possession while pursuing his researches. As Judge Bronson died in 1850, it was a piece of good fortune that this unique document did not completely disappear between that date and 1857, when his son discovered it. Doctor Bronson made such use of it as he wished in writing his History of the town, and in 1862 deposited it for safe-keeping with the New Haven Colony Historical Society."

In 1890, while Miss Prichard was at work upon her volume of "The Town and City of Waterbury," through the courtesy of Doctor Bronson, this Proprietors' Book came into her hands, and consisted at that time of twenty-six leaves, one having been lost since 1857.

It was in 1890 also that the discovery was made among the papers of the late John Kingsbury, Esq. (who was the last "Proprietors' Clerk"), by his grandson, Frederick J. Kingsbury, of the Articles of Association and Agreement, the writings of the Grand Committee, the two Indian deeds which form the illustrations of this volume, an almost complete record of the tax-lists of the town from 1730 to 1783, warnings to depart the town, and hundreds of deeds, agreements, and other valuable and interesting documents. All these papers were turned over to Miss Prichard for her use in writing the early history of Waterbury, and are now the property of the Mattatuck Historical Society.

As the Proprietors' Book stands, it contains the minutes of nearly seventy meetings, only two before 1689, and the last in 1722. A photograph of the manuscript as it came to Miss Prichard, showing the ragged cover and one of the pages, is reproduced in "The Town and City of Waterbury" (Vol. I., p. 216).

It has been submitted to the Emory process and bound in parchment, together with the extant records of the Grand Committee.

Mr. Kingsbury, in his memoranda for a preface,

refers to the "suggestions of a historic nature" to be found "in the leaves of this old record besides their written contents." He speaks of the paper as necessarily of English manufacture, mentions the noticeable variety in the inks that were used, and has a good deal to say about the chirography, some of which is "as clear and round and plain as the best handwriting of the present day," and "some in the scrawling hand of a man whose time was mostly spent in handling the hammer or the hoe, and whose spelling, even though he may have known better, was very apt to drop into the phonetic style." His added remark, that "some of it is phonetic to excess" may be verified by any one who glances at the following pages. One need not go further than the first page to discern the extraordinary variety and the apparent lawlessness of the orthography, and on page after page may be found instances that almost suggest inventive ingenuity on the part of these scribes of two centuries ago. We find prejudice spelled in at least ten different ways, the most notable occurring in the phrase, "pragadishing hy wais and fooremer grants." We find such combinations as "to met at twelf a klok," and "agarned till the seckond tousedday," and "spakticell pond," this last representing not an Indian name, but one of the Spectacle Ponds now included in Hamilton Park. We have also "gaufe" for gave, and "unannymus" and "to ragolat misstaks." But the chief struggle of the recorders seems to have been with the bachelors and their accommodations. Among the seven or eight different guises in which they appear, "bagelders" and "bacheldtors" are perhaps the most startling, although we have also "bagelders acomandation" and "bagilldors a coming dation." It will be seen also that striking variations of the same word occur on the same page and sometimes in the same sentence, showing that no rule of uniformity had been established or apparently thought of.

The remainder of the volume calls for little prefatory comment. At a meeting of the Proprietors held on November 27, 1722, "it was agreed by vote that the several acts of the Proprietors from this time forward shall be entered in the Town Book."

The acts of the Proprietors as thus recorded have been carefully copied from the Town Book, and constitute Part Third of this volume. The volume contains therefore a full record of the proceedings of the Waterbury Proprietors so far as it is possible to obtain it. On December 10, 1764, a vote was passed to have the old record book, then in Captain Thomas Porter's possession, "examined to see if anything should be copied." For many years after that vote, no record of the doings of the Proprietors appears, and as certain lay-outs of land are mentioned between 1764 and 1802, which refer to a division of Proprietors' rights made at certain dates, and no record is to be found of such division, it is thought that a volume of records must have been lost. There are also in the town records various entries in which the laying out of highways and some other matters are treated as acts of the town, although they were in fact acts of the Proprietors. These entries are not reproduced in this volume.

Parts Fourth and Fifth seem to call for no comment. The brief Appendix contains two papers which had been mislaid at the time Part First was printed.

Mr. Kingsbury's comments on the handwriting of the Proprietors' Book convey but a faint idea of the difficulties involved in the decipherment of some portions of the manuscript. The transcription of the text, some of it crowded and crabbed from the first, and blurred and stained and worn by age, has been achieved by the industry and expert skill of Miss Katharine A. Prichard, with the assistance of Mr. Benjamin F. Howland. The Index also is Miss Prichard's work.

Almost any one turning the leaves of this volume will find himself among the unused and obsolete place-names of an apparently unknown region. Yet we have here, although in disconnected passages and frag-mentary form, the record of the development of one of the most remarkable and most conspicuous of New England towns. While the genealogist finds in these pages a storehouse of materials in the form of family names, the sociologist and the historian may well study here, in its minutest manifestations, the unfold-ing of that community life which has given New England its fame and honor. And others, no doubt, who are proud of Waterbury, will prize the book as a remnant of the past, a souvenir that cannot be duplicated.

JOSEPH ANDERSON.

January 24, 1911.

CONTENTS

Waterbury Proprietors' Records

Orders and Letters of the "General Court's Committee for the Settling of Mattatuck." October 9, 1673—September 9, 1687.

October. 9: 1673

P 39:[1] In. answer to the petis on to saver all inhabytants of the town of farmingtown that matatuck that thos lands may be granted for a plantation: this cort have sen caus to order that thos lands may be veiued som tim betwen this and the cort in may next: and that re port may be made to the cort in may next: whe. it be judged fit to make a plantation the committy apointed are Lt thomas Ball: Lt Robert Webster and Dannill Pratt

A True Copy of Record

Test HEZ: WYLLYS Secry

May the: 14: 1674

p. 45: the committy apointed by the general cort for the veiuing of. mattatuck return that they judg it a sutabul plas to acomydat thurty famylis this cort nomynat and apoint Major John Talcut: Lef Robbert Webster Lef. Nichlis Omsted Insin Samuel Stell Insin John Wadsworth to be a committy to regulat and order the setling of a plantation att matitack in the most sutabul way that may be:

A True Copy of Record

Test HEZ: WYLLYS Secry.

[1] Records of the General Court of Conn. Vol. II. The original documents are to be found in "Towns and Lands, Vol. I."

At a meeting of the Committee for Mattatuck Jany
15, 1677: it was agreed and Concluded./.

MSS   That wee do accept of Johne Roote Senr sub-
scribing to the Articles for settling of mattatuck, in
the behalfe of one of his sonnes, and we accept of
John Scovel on Acc^t of Abraham Brunson, and
Benjamin Barnes on Acc^t of Richard Seemer. and of
John Standly Junr for Joseph Gaylor on the Acc^t of
Thomas Gridly, Subscribeing to submit to the Article
a fore sayd dated May 30th 1674, and in soe doeing
are accepted as inhabitants of the place. David
Carpenter subscribing in behalfe of John porter is
accepted upon the same Terms.|.

2   Wee do order that all necessary High wayes for
the Towns use, are to be mended suffitiently, at the
charge of the meadow alottments, according to the
Third Article, for settlement of Mattatuck dated
May 30th 1674: the three great lotts only only Accepted,
and desire and appoint Benjamin Jud to call out the
proprietors in their turnes for doing their Just part
and in this service of a surveigho^r to attend the
Country Law.|

3.   We do alsoe allow the proprieto^rs of Mattatuck
one year for settleing them selves on the fore s^d Mattatuck, more than was first granted, notwithstanding
anything to the Contrary, and all publique charges
to be born one year longer, or more, than is concluded
in the third Article Dated May 30th *1677*. (1674)
notwithstanding any thing there in Signified to ye
Contrary.

4   Wee do allow all necessary High wayes for the
use of the inhabitants that may be needfull, to be
layd out by such as we shall appoint, whiles we are
in power, and afterwards the Town to stake and lay

out Such High wayes or Common passages as shall by them be Juded necessary.|.

5 Wee order the Highway of sixteen rods wide that is already layd out North and South through the old Town plott to be but Two rods wide, and grant that the proprietors of each side the sayd High way to abbut upon the sayd now Highway for enlargm^t of their lott proportionally.

6 wee order the common fence on the east side of the River for secureing the meadows shall be made suffitiently by the last of May, proportionally according to the Number of Acres of meadow Land each propriator is seized off, and we desire and appoint, William Judd Thomas Judd, and John Standly to protion the sayd fence, and lay out each person his Just dues, and being so layd out each person that shall neglect makeing his Just proportion, shall be fineable according to ye Law of this Colony.|.

JOHN TALCOTT
JOHN WADSWORTH
NICHO OLMSTEAD
SAMUELL STELE

[On the reverse of this paper
is the drawing of the old
Town Plot lots.]

March 11th 167^8/$_9$

1 We the Committee for Mattatuck or the Majo^r part of us being mett, according to Joynt agreement, at Farmington and taking sundry matters into consideration, have determined That Lieu^t Stanley with the helpfullness of William Judd, and John Standly Junr shall lay out those Lotts to the proprietors of

mattatuck that are not yet done, they granting sutable allowance for their paines and Labo[r] therein.

2 Whereas there is a mile of fence, or there abouts, yet to be errected for secuering those Landes that are under improvement: from ye spoyle of Cattle and swine, wee do advise and order, that William Judd Thomas Judd and John Standly Jun[r] shall proportion and Stake out to each proprietor his proportion, with all speed, conveniant.

3 Wee further order, that each proprieto[r] do errect a suffisent fence upon those respective places appointed, for defence of that Land, that noe damage bee done to either Corn or grass, by Cattle or Swine, which fence shall be done betwixt this and the first of May next.

4 And its o[rd] erd[e] That Liut: Samuel Steel william Judd and John Standly Jun[r] lay out to the proprietors their Three Acre Lotts that are granted to them, according to former agreem[t]

5 And whereas William Judd had a grant, that his Three Acre Lott should be Layd out upon the west end of his House Lott, it is ordered that it be so layd out and recorded to him

JOHN TALCOTT./.

Pr us JOHN WADSWATH

NICHO OLMSTEAD

[THE THREE-ACRE LOTS.]

Thee order which is the adition of the hous Loots in maticok as it is too be tackan up

thos that desire too tack up their adition in the rere of theere house Loots we shall doe all that we can too acomidat ach man in that partuckuller too be suted −first and 2−3− so goe on in that order

1   benjamun barnes
2   Samuell he cok
3   Joseph he cok
4   John willton
5   abriham andrus
6   benjiman Judd
7   John bronson
8   will higisan for will higisne piched north sid of
    sam Judd
9   Thomas nuill
10 Thomas hankocks
11 Samuill Judd
12 John nuill To reseive 2 akers at the rer of his lot
13 grat Loot next Tho richison piched for the greet
    Lot south side roring rivier part buting at John
    caringtons est
14 Tho Richason
15 adward scott too reseive his loot at the east side
    of the roring river.
16 John carrington
17 benjamin Jones ben Jons south sid roring river
    next to that I piched at for ye great lot
18 [. . . . .]
19 david carpentore piched for david carpenter [. . . . .]
    Tho hankkox if he like it
20 Themothy Standly   piched for themothy standly
    at the south of Tho richisons if he like it
21 danill Porter
22 John Judd   for John Judd north side of John
    warners lot roring river if he like it.
23 Tho Judd
24 John Standly to reseive achur more
25 John Scovill
26 John Lanchton piched south of Thimothi standly

27 obadiah richards
28 Great lot next abriham andrus
29 Thomas warner
30 Isack bronson to reseive 2 akers end of his lot
31 John warner
     Danill warners next to John warners
32 Joseph gallar
33 great loot est end

May '79 the planters of Matuck being at the towne plot aded by vote Thomus Judd too William Judd John standly and Sam Stell too equilize the Lande too lay ought in the divishun of Land from manhan medows upward and mack adishun too thos lots in that devishun acording too the quality of the land and remoteness of it as the fore said partys shal judg to be just and right

The first meadow	20 ackers	
The second	33 ackers	53
The third west sid river	21	
4 medow	6 ackers	27
Est sid river the first meadow from the		
south 12 ackers	Island 5 ackers	17
2 meadow est side 23 ackers		23
		120

DEVISTION OF LAND AND FENS
MANHAN AND STEELS MEDOW

The devistion of the secnd remayndeer of the Land in manhan medow and Stells medow and ben Juds medow and hanckocks medow and at the small brocke as foloweth

we furst begin furst at manhan meadow and 2
in hancoks medow 3 at a bit of land at the west
side of the river aganst hanckkoks medow 4 at the
south end of the broock aganst hanckoks medow 5 at
the lower end of the land which lys at the broock which
coms downe in too Stells medow and gos upward and
end at the north end of ben Juds medow at willum
higisuns Loot and acording too this order too draw
lots twoo ackers for a hundred pound and if thes
Lands herein exprest fall short of This devetion then
too be made up by any undevided lands axsept this bit
of Lande calld a pastors—

We begin in hanckoxs meadow at The southward
end of That bit at the west sid of the river aganst
hankox meadow at the south end

The Loots as they fell in this divishon in or by
drawing

		ackers	half-ackers	rods
1	John Bronson	1	half	16
2	Joseph gayllor	1	half	32
3	Tho Warner	2	00	00
4	edmun Scot	2	00	00
5	obidiah richards	1	half	16
6	danill warner	1	00	32
7	John nuill	2	00	00
8	Tho hancocks	2	00	00
9	John warner	1	03 roods	3
10	grat Lott	3	00	00
11	John Carriton	1	00	32
12	ben Jones	2	00	00
13	Samuill hecok	1	a haf	32
14	will higison	1	1 rood	24
15	John willton	1	haf	16
16	Tho nuill	1	3 roods	8
17	benja Judd	1	3	3

		ackers	half-ackers	rods
18	John Lanckton	2	00	00
19	isack bronson	1	3 roods	3
20	John Judd	2	00	00
21	Tho richison	1	00	00
22	abriham andros	1	haf	16
23	grat loot	3	00	00
24	grat loot	3	00	00
25	John Scovill	1	haf	16
26	david Carpinder	1	haf	16
27	John Standly	2	00	00
28	daniell porter	1	3 roods	3
29	willam judd	2	00	00
30	timothy standly	1	3 roods	24
31	Joseph hecox	1	00	32
32	ben barns	2	00	00
33	Samuill Judd	1	haf	16
34	Tho Judd	2	00	00

At a meeting of the Committee for Mattatuck on the 26st of November 1679./.

Whereas we have received information by some of the inhabitants belonging to that place that many of the propriators to home allotments were granted have hitherto neglected setlmt of themselves and familyes there, to the great discouragement and weakening the hands of those that are already upon the place with their familyes.

We have thought meet to determin and resolve, that all such proprietors as shall not be personally with there familyes inhabitting at Mattatuck by the Last of May next insueing and there to abide, shall forfeit all their right, title, propriety and intrest, in any Allotments granted to them at mattatuck, to be dissposed by the Committee to such others as they shall approve off. Allsoe we do further determin, that all such inhabitants as shall not errect a mansion house, by the last of May come Twelve months, according to a former Articles to that purpose, shall forfeit all there rights and title in Lands at Mattatuck as a fore sayde.

Pr us
{ JOHN TALCOTT:
JOHN WADSWORTH
NICHO: OLMSTEAD
SAMUELL STELL

Farmington, Novemb^r 26: 1679

Whereas Daniel warner with his family were upon the remove to mattatuck, and on that juncture of time, the divine providence of god hath removed the sayd Daniel out of the Land of the Liveing.

out of compassion to his relict and children Left behinde him, we do grant the sayd Relict shall hould her Allotments firme and good to her selfe and children, notwithstanding anything conteyned in any former Article to the Contrary, only advising her selfe and relationes that a dweling House be errected there with all posible speed, and that she in habit there, or some suffitient person to manage her Lands and Accommodations upon the place.

Pr us
{ JOHN TALCOTT
JOHN WADSWORTH
NICH: OLMSTEAD
SAMUELL STELL

Farmington, November 27 1679   At a meeting of the Committee for Mattatuck.

It is determined that that High way Layd out by Lieu^t Saml Steel at the east end of the Town plat at of mattatuck, running eastward out of sayd Town plat being Three rods wide, shall awayes be and remayne for publick and common use, which is between Joseph Gaylers Lott and a Hous Lott reserved for such inhabitant as shall hereafter be entertayned.

Alsoe it is agreed and determined that the House Lott of Two Acres lying at the east end of the Town abutting northerly on Thomas Warners Hous Lott and a piece of meadow and swamp contayning about fifteen Acres by estimation lying upon Steels Brook, abutting upon the North on Edman Scott Junie[r] on Thomas Judd Jun[r] on the east, and on a hill south and west. And a peice of Land conteyning by estimation Three Acres, lying in the pasture Land commonly so called, shall be and remayne for the use, occupation and improvem[t] of the Ministery of the sayd Town forever, without any alteration or dissposall use or improvement: whatsoever.

For encouragem[t] of an inhabitant we do agree and grant that an additional House Lott to what was formerly allowed be Layed out, and a Three Acre Lott and eight Acres in the new devision to be Layd out, and eight Acres at the old Town plot and Ten Acres upon a playn on the west side of Steels Meadow is granted, and about Twelve Acres if it will upon tryall prove so much, and be not already dissposed, lying on the Southern end of Buck Meadow being an Island allwayes provided that such person as shall be excepted to be free of the sayd A llo ttment shall subscribe to the Articles formerly made

we do advise the inhabitants of Mattatuck to build a suffitient Corn mill, for the use of the Town, and keep the same in good repration for that work and service of grinding Corne, and for encouragem[t] we grant such persons shall have Thirty Acres of Land Layd out and shall be and remain to them and their heirs and assignes for ever, he or they mayntayning the sayd grist mill as afore sayd forever.

We allow the standing of Thomas warners celler without molestation according to agreement: of Liu^t sam^{ll} Stelle.

NICHO OLMSTED: JOHN TALCOTT
SAMUELL STELL   JOHN WADSWORTH

THE DEVISTION TO THE STRAITS.
[1679]

The order which is agreed of in the deviding of and drawing of Loots for thos Landes which Lyith downe the river from those Landes allrady Layed ought too the rivurit which runnith in too The rivur on the est side of The river at the straytes and also a madow which is up the river from the towne plot called by the name of boock medow and in the deviding of the abouf said lands we agree that three roods of the best of this Land shall be accounted as one acker and the worst of the Land which we devide shall be acounted sevine roods but for one acker and so rys and fall in this division acording too the goodnes or badness of this Lande and this to be considered and equilized by thos which are or shall Laye ought this foresaid land in too ther severall alotments and all so we agree that there shall be fiufe ackers alowd too a hundred pound a lot ment and if thes Lands apoynted too this devision shall falle short too alowe acording too this proportion too aviry alotment then thos which fall short too tack up thar proporshon in any undevided medow axsept a pes of Land caled the pastur or a pasall of Land which lyith at the

broock which runith in too Stells madow and in this
devision this foresaid Land from the broock abutith
at willum higisons Loot north and at Thomas Juds
Land est and in this devition it shall be in the power
of The abof said persons if they se resone so too doe too
throwe in Landes in Too thos Sevarall alotments and
count it not in the masher acording to ther decresion
and we begin in this devision first at the south side of
the rivur and the Loots too rune south and north
which we count up and downe the river and the furst
Loot in order too be acounted that next the river and
so rune downe the medow too the strayts and tack the
lots in order as they falle at the north end and at the
strayts rune over the river at the est side of the river
in lick maner and goo upward and ende at the devided
Land at the fore saide side and then goo up in too
books medow and begin in that alotment at the southward or lower end and goo upward and end at the
upur side or ende of that madow

The lots as they fall by suckseson

	greatt lote—	1		John langton—	14
	abram andrus—	2		John newell—	15
	John Carington—	3		Benjamen Jons—	16
	benjamen barns—	4	85	Samuell hikoc—	17
	John wilton—	5	90	John warner—	18
	william Judd—	6	80	Samuel Judd—	19
	John Judd sener—	7	60	Danell warner—	20
	willum higson—	8	95	Timothy standly—	21
	Daved Carpenter—	9		benjamin Judd—	22
80	Josep gayler—	10		Thomas warner—	23
	John Scovell—	11	90	Danell porter—	24
	Edman Scootte—	12	90	Izacke brownson—	25
50	Thomas richason—	13	60	Josep hiscox—	26

90 Thomas newell—	27	Obadiah Richards—	31
Thomas Judd—	28	Thomas hancox—	32
John Standly—	29	John brownson—	33
ye lote Botte—	30	great lote—	34

At a meeting of the Committee for Mattatuck
Febry: 5th 1680 at Farmington.

It was then determined by us, that those Town offi-
cers that wear chosen by ye inhabitants of s^d Mattatuck shall execute their respectieve offices and that
for the future the inhabitants of the place being orderly
called and convented by their Majo^r voat shall have
liberty to chose their Townsmen constables surveigho^rs
fenc viewers and Haywards or any other civel officers
from time to time without any further order from y^e
Committee.

It is further concluded that stephen Hopkins who
hath built a mill at that plantation shall have that
Thirty Acres appointed and intailed in a former order
to such as shall errect a mill there and so much more
Land added to the sayd Thirty Acres as may advance
the same to be in value of one hundred pounds alottment.

And in consideration of some of those persons that
have had a Lottments Granted at Mattatuck we have
heard the alligations layd in against them and do
determin that Deacon John Lancton, William Judd,
and David Carpenter have forfeited all their rights
and titles to those a Lottments granted to them at
Mattatuck not haveing attended those Articles to
which they have subscribed.

Just here it is agreed by us that in case any shall
appere desireing a Lottments there, shall subscribe to

the originall Articles and engage allsoe to errect a
dwelling House according to dimensions, set down in
sayd Articles within one year after subscription and
settled with his or their familyes upon the place within
that time, otherwise to forfeit all their grant of Lands
and right, theirin, to be dissposed to such others as
the Committee shall Judg meet.

It was allsoe agreed that all Leavyes for defraying
the public charges of that plantation, shall be raysed
upon the meadow Alottments, according to a former
Article and so to stand from this day to the Last of
Feb^{r}y: in ye year 1682 whatching and warding only
excepted.

Upon further considerations we have hereby granted
that Benjamin Judd and Isaac Brunson shall have so
much uplands added to their Allotmts: as shall make
their meadow alottments in value of one hundred
poundes, and that sayd Addission, to be added to their
respective eight Acre allotments allready granted.

And whereas Daniel Port^r and Thomas Richason
make complaynt that they are in want of Land to
improve, we grant liberty to the Town to add to what
they have, according to their good disscretion, and
what shall be allowed by the Town, shall be layd out
to them by Benjamin Judd and John Standly, and
allsoe to lay out what belongeth to ye mill, and Miller.
Wee do order what fences is necessary to be made
for secureing Lands under improvem^t: shall be speedily
proportioned and layd out by Thomas Judd John
Standly and the present Townsmen and the same to
be made by ye Last of Aprell next.

And whereas Stephen Upson maketh complaynt
that he is much streightened, in his present possession
of Lands, we grant an addission according to what the

Town shall se cause to be Layd out by him, by Tho: Judd John Standly and the present Townsmen. There is allsoe a House Lott, contayneing in estimat^n: Two Acres granted to Stephen Hopkins, as conveniantly as may bee to sute the mill, and the fore sayd Thomas Judd John Standly and the present Townsmen to lay it out to him and allsoe a Three Acre lott according as the other in Habitants have granted to be layd out by the same persons. for him.

Allsoe we do grant Benjamin Judd shall have added to the North end of his House Lott some land to build on, allwayes provided that the High way that runeth Through ye Town in that place shall be and and remayne foure Rods and halfe wide, to be layd out to him by the fore sayd persons.

Pr us $\left\{\begin{array}{l} \text{JOHN TALCOTT} \\ \text{JOHN WADSWORTH} \\ \text{NICHO OLMSTEAD} \end{array}\right\}$ Coommittee

Hartford May 22 1680

William Judd Thomas Judd, and John standly, these are to give your selves or such others as y^{or} inhabitants of Mattatuck shall see cause to appoint, to be a Committee to meet with confer, and consult any person or persons appointed by o^r Hon^d ffriends of woodbery, as their Committee impowered, to agree and conclude of and determin a Bounde Lyne twixt you, and what you shall do therein shall be well accepted by yor Loveing ffriends.

JOHN TALCOTT

JOHN WADSWORTH

May 31,
1680

ttheyes are to sertyfi our

friends att wodbury: or whom
ytt may conserne that we the
Inhabitants of matatock do
not se caus to apointe any other
persons as a comite but
aquies in that apointed by yor
comite: and m^r wadsworth to
mete with agree and conclude and determin a
boundery betwixte: may the 31, 1680:
John wellton Samuell hickcox
in the behalfe of the reste

Hartford, May 22, 1680
To o^r ffriends at Mattatuck

We, understanding that yor meadows and improuv-
mts therein Ly upon spoyle by cattle and swin, have
been necessitated to come to an agreement to determin
the doeing of Thre hundred and fifty Rods of new
Fence to run from the north end of what is done,
northerly without which it seems much damage will
come upon the propretors of yor feildes.

These are therefore to impower Thomas Judd, John
Standly, Sam^{ll} Hecoks or any other with them whome
you shall think meet, to Lay out and proportion the
above sayd fence to each proprietor belonginge to the
sayd meadows or fields and that it be done forthwith,
and we order that whatsoever proprieto^r shall not have
errected a suffitient fence by the Tenth of June next,
shall upon disstreynt pay six pence ye Rod and the
same summe ye Rod for every week after sayd Tenth
of June, untill it shall be Adjued by yor towne mesurer
to be suffitient, to be delivered for the use of the Town.

Pr us { JOHN TALCOTT
           JOHN WADSWORTH.

Complants of severall men not building
acording to artyculs [Feb. 1682.]

Benja Jud challenged for Breach of Articles in not
comeing to mattatuck in 8̄o: Test: Isaac Brunson,
Dan¹ port^{er} & Stephen Upson that he came not at
ye time prefixed   2^d his not building according to
Articles as time, but It was done in 8̄1: in September
and withdrawn oft from ye place.

Samuel Judd not built according to time prefixed
He built and went into his House in Novemb^{er} 8̄1: and
not fit before Test: Steph: upson   it was shingled
about michaelmuss Test: Dan^{ll} Porter, Test Isaac
Brunson

Thomas Hancoks hath a House covered allmost all
and clabborded and noe chimney—within the time
stated.   Test: Samuel Hecoks John Scovel and Isaac
Brunson.   disserted the place being gone all or ye
greatest of the year past.

Timothy Standly and Joseph Gaylerd their Housen
Big enough: and ovned

Jno Carrington House not Large enough: according
to Articles.

Cooper Andrews noe House

Tho: Nuel came not according Articles neither Built
according to Articles & House not finished

Daniel porter noe chimney to his House according
to Articles.

Tho: warner House not built according to Articles
for time not finished.

Tho: Richison noe House lives in a ciller, only hires
a Ciller to live in.

Edward Scott Junr noe chimny to His House.

Obediah Richards not Built his House not according
to the demension of it.

2

The Town desires taxsation to be Layed on Lands
for some further Time

Benjamin Joanes complayned of for neglect of
cohabitation.

John Nuel complayned of for ye same.

John Scovl noe chimny.

[E?] d Scott complais

At a meeting of the Committy for Mattatuck
at Farmington, Feb^{r}y: the sixt in the yeare 1682.
Wee haveing heard the Complaynts; and Alligations
of Serg^t Thomas Judd, and Serg^t John Standly and
other Friends sent from Mattatuck, as persons impowered to implead sundry of the proprietors there,
for that they have not errected their dwelling Housen,
and finished the same, according to provission and
enjunction by Articles concluded; by the Committee
for Mattatuck, Novembe^r 26: 1679.

Upon what pleas and proofs have presented, wee
do Adjudg and Condemn all the granted allotments
formerly layd out to Benjamin Jud, Samuel Judd, and
Thomas Hancox, to be by us condemned as Forfeited,
and thereon disclaime there former right had or might
have had therein.

And it is further by us agreed and determined, that
whosover shall hereafter have grants from o^{ur} selves
to be seized or put into the possession of their grants as
proprietors and inhabitants at s^d Mattatuck, shall be
engaged and firmly Bound by this Act, to reside and
dwell in s^d Mattatuck, the full terme and time of four
yeares, in a steddy way and mañer with their Familyes,
after subscription to this Act and order and in case
those mancion Housen on those Lands allready errected

cannot be bought at a resonable rate of the present
owners by such as shall be seized of their Allotments,
or in case of non agreement about the price or prizes of
s^d Buildings, the person or persons that shall subscribe
to this act and order, shall errect and make mantion
Housen according to the Articles for that purpose
made in 30th of May: in the yeare 1674.—and upon
default or non performance of either of the Two parts
of this determination, such person or persons neglecting
to Build within the spare time or Terme of four yeares
after subscription, or faile of cohabitting on the place as
a fore sayd, shall forfeit all right and title in such lands
or alottments they or he shall be seized off, and in case
those friends whose lands are at this meeting by us
condemned, do desire to be repossessed of their present
Lands condemned as forfeited, shall subscribe to this
present Act and order, in case we see reason to reposses
him on them. And this Act and order; to be of force
in referance to David Carpenters Lott formerly Condemned. And whereas Timothy Stanly, Joseph Gaylerd, John Carrington, Abraham Andrus Cooper,
Thomas Nuel, Daniel Porter, Thomas warner, Thomas
Richison, Obediah Richards, and John Scovel, for
their not Building, and some of the fore sayd not cohabitting according to Articles to that purpose made
p^r the Committee May 30th, 1674, wee do by these
Adjudg and condemn their Allotments to be forfeited
yet notwithstanding upon their submission and refor-
mation, with their cohabitation upon the place one
compleat year, as addissionall to the four yeares
injoyned in that Article made to that purpose in May
30th, 1674, otherwise this present condemnation to
stand in full force. In referance to defraying all publick charges by Levys or Rate, it is granted to be done

and Layd upon Lands as formerly for the Two past
years following the date hereof and the charges of
makeing and mending of Highwayes by the same.

It is Granted that each proprietor as addition all to
their former grants, shall each inhabitant have eight
Acres p^r man, layd out to them in such places within
their Town Bounds as the inhabitants shall agree, to be
layd out by persons chosen by ye inhabitants of the
place.

And in referance to ye Act of the inhabitants of
Mattatuck granting Samuel Hecox an addission of
Land as by a coppy of their records appeares, we the
committee give o^{ur} consent and confirme the same to
him.

In referance to what lands are granted by the
inhabitants of Mattatuck, to John Hopkins the present
miller, we do well approve off, and in case they shall
see cause to ease the intayle of any part of the $\frac{lb}{100}$
Allotment, we shall not object against it. Upon the
pettition of Serg^t Jno Stanly that he may be accom-
modated with four or five Acres of Meadow Land up
the River although it be four or five miles off from the
Town, in consideration of the meaness of his Allotments, wee the Committee do advise the inhabitants
to a complyance thereunto.

The foregoeing conclusiones signed Feb^{r}y 7th, 1682.

Pr us { JOHN TALCOTT
        JOHN WADSWORTH   } Committee for
        NICHO: OLMSTEAD }   Mattatuck

At Farmington, Feb^{r}y seaventh 1682 Edward
Scott senio^r Did personally appeare, and
did publickly, freely and fully declare that
he did give and grant to his son Edward

Scott Junr that House set for a dwelling House on the Home Lott granted to his sayd son by mattatuck committee, and all his rights in those other Land granted by sayd Committee belonging to that Home Lott on which sayd House now stands, with all the charges and expences thereon, and what he hath disburst for sayd Lands in reference to the purchase thereof, to be and remaine, to his sayd son, to him and his Heires forever, without any further or future clayme, from him selfe or from any other by or under him.

| wee the Committee grant phillip Judd the quiet possession of that Land and allotments at Matta-tuck | the above said was fully signified and declared befor us
JOHN TALCOTT
JOHN WADSWORTH } Asst. |

that was formerly his Broth Samuel Judds lands this 13th of June, 1687.

Pr us JOHN TALCOTT
JOHN WADSWORTH } Committee

we hose names ar here under wrighten do subscrib to a faithfull submission and observation of the act of the committee one the other sid of this lefe, Feby th
6–1682

Subscribed this 4 June 83 Thomas hancox
Janiwari 10 83 THOMAS JUDD JUNER
May 26 = 84 ROBERT PORTER
June 13 = 87 PHILIP JUDD

Hartford, Jan'y: the 10th, 1683:

Thomas Judd Juni^r is accepted as an inhabitant at Mattatuck   his father Thomas Judd haveing signified his desires of the same he the sayd Thomas Judd Junr subscribeing to the Act and order of the Committee Febuary the sixt, 1682. in referance to benjamine Juds allotment, and privilidg of reseizen of the same upon condissiones in the sayd Act and order granted.   It being determined by us the Committee, in case any grant or grantes be made by the inhabitants of Mattatuck, to Thomas Judd Junr in referance to possession of any parcells or Tracts of Land is hereby made voyd and of none effect, notwithstanding any thing to the Contrary.   And whereas there is an Addission formerly granted by the Committee to Benjamin Judds home Lott, it is now ordered that the sayd Addission shall not be run further into the High way then it was layd   by Serg^t Jn° Stanly Thomas Judd and the Townsmen appointed for that service.

Pr us   JOHN TALCOTT
         JOHN WADSWORTH
         NICHO OLMSTEAD   } Committee
         SAMUEL STELL, SENR

To the Select men of Waterberi

Gentel men, when we had the last meting at farmington, conserning your afayers it was pleaded and owned by sum of youre selfes that there was a devision of land layd out where in it was agreed by youre self and the Committee that layed it out that there should be an aditione namely ⅘ for one acare that is to say part of that devision but thorow forgetfull nes or over sitt it was ometed, and soe the persons conserned fall short of what they should have had   this Is there fore to Request and desier you to acomodat those persons conserned with that which may be just one the fore mensined acount and so as they may be suted as well as you can, for without dout they will be lousers by not haveing it together with fore sd devesion which Is all at present from him who is youer asuerd frind and sarvant

JOHN WADSWORTH

poscript youer atendent to the above sd shall be alowed by us the Committee, farmington Sept. 9. 1687.[1]

[1] This, the latest of the Committee's papers, is in form a letter, upon which the broken seal remains, showing two curved arrows pointing downward.

Addressed
To the
Select men of
Waterbery this.

All that remains of the
Original Proprietors' Book
May 21, 1677—October 31, 1722.

First Proprietors' Book.

At a metinge held by the propriators of Matatucke may the twenty first 1677 upon furder Consideration of some difeculty that doth atend them seting the towne whare It is now layd out theay made chois of Deacon Judde John Langhton senor, John Andrus seanr goodman Rote and John Judde and Danell porter as a Comite to vew and consider whether It will not be more for the benefit of the propriators In Genarall: to set the towne on this Este side of the River contenting themselfes with les hom lots provided: thos formerly layde out be secured to them: provided also they thincke and conclude It so to be to advis with the grande Comite and in conjunction with them they giveinge liberty so to doe we the proprietors agre to act Acordingly not withstanding what is alredy done[1]

March the 21 1686: we whose names are herafter subscribed beinge desired and apointed by the towne to state what fens shall be and remaine to the minesters lote: determin as followeth: northwarde from the towne the devison of fens between John wilton and the widow warners: 2 devison between Thomass Judds smith and

[1] The first layout was on "Town Plot" so called for that reason. In consideration of danger from Indians and from being cut off from Farmington, their base of supplies, by flood, they decided to change the layout.

27

timothy standly: against hancox medow and the 3d
to be the upermost in the new devison

the fourth devision att the north end of copers
fens at the made medow 5 devison atwien goodman
richardson and edman scot Junor against the longe
medow.

THOMAS JUDD SENER
JOHN STANDLY
SAMUELL HICKCOX

Jan the 21 1689   wheras att a meeting of the propriators of waterbury: we whos nams are underwriten
doe ingage to bare the Damage that shall be done in the
felds granted to us to fens in to ceep swine: we say the
damag that shall be done either by [swine] that rune
in the Coman not yocked or ringed: or any sorts of
horses and catle exept any shall put any hogs or cattle
into the felds purposly: that is to say each man to bare
his own damag that is done in thes felds

STEPHEN UPSON his ⌐ ⌐marrke
SAMUEL SCOOTE his S marrke
RICHARD PORTER

the number of acrs in the small medows up the
river and at wosters swamp preparde for the last
divison:

Att worsters swamp   46 acrs _____ 46
1 Att the uper end of the bounds: on the
  west sid the river in the first medow
  and ajasente   18 acrs   18
2 second aight and a halfe _____ 8½
3 in a strips that rune by the river to the
  mouth of the brooke and up the brooke
  above twich gras medow — — — — 6

4 twich gras medow	_____	4½

plains a bove Ensen Judds Iland with the	⁵ ⁶	
hill sid pines ———————		6 34
pin medow _____		7–0

from the uper end 1 bounds on the Est

1 sid and so downward att the plom tres ____	2 acrs
2 in a small med _____	2½
3 in another med _____	4
4 pople medo _____	10½
5 against Judds Ialand _____	6
6 Jeroco _____ _____ _____	4

up the west branch uper or west branch:

nor sid	5	acrs
west sid "	11	
south sid	2	
north sid	8	
north 3	3	

Att a meetting of the propriators of Watterbury, January the 21: 1689 the propriators granted Steven Upson seven acrs and Samuell Scoote seven acrs that is to say 14 acrs between them of land upon the hill Estward of the path from the longe wigwam upon the hill: to be layed in a hansom forme: for a hoge feld provided itt doo not predyedes former grants thay to bare the damage shall be done acording to the articles to which they have subscribed

Att the same meeting ther was granted richard porter seven acrs: agasent to the above said lands granted to Steven upson and Samuell Scoote provided he fens and improve itt in four yere or els it shall returne to the use of the propriators and to performe the conditions to which he hath subscribed being a hog feld

At the sam meting the proprietors granted to
Samuell hickox sn seaven a cers of land on the hill on
the west side of hoog pound broke on the same condistion richard porter had his

at the same meting theay granted John wellton
sn seaven acers on the same condistion that is to say
buting on samuell hickox

at the sam meting theay granted to thomas Judd sn
seaven acers of land on the hill with samll hickox

at the same meting the proprietors granted Edman
scot sn seaven acers of land with them on the same
hill

at the same meting the proprietors granted to
timothy standly and obedyah Richards fourteen acers
of land on the hill whear samuell hickox pitched for his
hogg feeld: to mak hoog feld

at the same meting the proprietors granted to
thomas Judd the smith seaven acers of land on the hill
samuel hickox is granted on: for hoog feld

at the same meting the proprietors granted to
thomas warner and danill warner, edman scot Ju
twenty one acers of land on the west side of the bever
pond brook buting on thomas warners eaight acer lot
for hoog feld

at the same meting the proprietors granted Isaac
brunson and benjamin barns fourteen acers of land on
the hill on the est side of hoog pound brooke and on the
north side of the rood that leds to farmington for a
hoog feld

at the sam meting the proprietors granted to
abraham andrus sn seaven acers of land with Isaac
brunson for hoog feld

Att the same meting the proprietors granted m^r
Jerimiah peck and his soon Jerimiah fourteen acers of

land at the south east end of turcy hill to run a booth
sids of the brook

Att the sam meting the propriators granted to
Abraham Andros juner sevn acers of land joyning to
m^r pecks land at turcy hill

these aboofe writen grants are to be one the same
condistions as richard porters grant was granted

Att a meting of the proprietors of Waterbury gen-
wary 21 1689 ther was granted to Thomas Richardson
six acers of land in the swamp and Lo Lands one the
west sid of his boogey meadow on the old town
plat.

At the same meting the propriators granted Edman
Scoot Senor four acers of Land on the west sid of
Thomas hancoxs eyght acer Lot provided it pregedis
not former grants: he reLinquishing his grant at
wigwam swamp

At the same meting the proprietors granted to John
warner four acers of Land at the east end and north
east corner of his three acer Lot: not to pregidish highways:

at the same meting the proprietors granted thomas
judd ju foure acers of land on the north side and este
end of his foure acer lot.

at the same meting the proprietors granted to John
scovell Ju a pese of land buting on John warners three
acer lot on the est on a hy waye on the west and south
and on thomas Judd Ju on the north provided he bild
a hous acording to origanall artyculs and coinhabit
four yers after

at the same meting the proprietors granted to gorg
scoot thre acers of land on the nor est side of the land

belonging to the estat of robberd porter and on the west side of the path being in two pessis provided it dont pregidish hy way and former grants

at the same meting the proprietors grantid to jonythan scoot a pees of land buting on a hywaye on the est on john hopkins on the north on thomas warner and passinig land on the west on the south on steven upsons land and to build a hous acording to origenal artycles and inhabit four yers

at the sam meting the proprietors grantid to ephrem warner a pes of land buting on north west south on a hy waye and on thomas Judd sn three acer lot on the est provided he build a hous acording to origenal artycels and coinhabit foure yers after

at the same meting the proprietors granted to Timothy Standley foure acers of land to jine to his foure acere lot one the west side of the river buting on the south and est side and end provided he relink quish foure acers of his eaight acer devistion formerly granted

at the same meting the proprietors granted to Isaac brumson foure acers of land on the south end of the burnt hill buting on thomas richason land on the south and to run from the brow of the hill up the litell brooke and to spring este ward of thomas richasons lot if he se case: provided he relinkquish a former grant of a four acer lote

at the sam meting the proprietors granted to John brumson a pese of land about two acers halfe on the nor west sid of his four acer lot in bens medow

at the sam meting the proprietors granted to John Judd four acers of land on the est sid of his fathers six acere and thre acer lot and so swing est ward: for paster land:

at a meting of the proprietors of Waterbury Jene 21
1689 there was grantid to John Richards foure acers of
land buting on John Judd on the west danil warners
three acer lot on the est on hy waye south: provided he
buld house with in four yers: and co in habit four yers

att the same metting ther was granted to John
Standly and abraham andrus a try angle pess that
lyeth betwen their land on the west side the river on
the west sid of abrams aight acre lote:

Att the same meeting the propriators granted
John Standly to acers att Jerico of upland in the valy
up the hill on the north side of his medow land toward
the north corner of his medow lote and to fling in the
hill to join it to his other lote:

Att the same meeting the propriators granted
obadiah richards a pes south west ward from the long
meadow that the path runes through provided it doe
not pregadis high-ways: one acre

[Although the meeting of January 26, 1691, follows
upon the same page with the preceding, these entries
regarding Mr. Peck, which are upon a small bit of
paper, properly belong here.]

Att a meeting of the propriators of Watterbury
march the 18: 1689 they did unanimusly desire m^r
Jerimy pecke Senr of grinage to setle with them in the
worke of the minestry:

Att the same meeting for the encoragment of m^r
Peck Above said: the propriators gave him the house
built for the minester with the hom lote att his first
Entranc there with his famely

Att the same meetting the above said propriators of
waterbury granted: Mr Jerimy peck of grinage the

other alotments or sevarall devisions belonging to the
minesters lot so caled provided he Cohabite with them
four yers and if the providens of god so Dispos that he
shold Dye befor the four yers be out itt shall fall to his
heirs:

Att the same meetinge the propriators granted to
Calebe and Jerimy peeke the to hous lots layd out to
the great lots on buting westerly on abraham and rus his
hom lot the other on ben Jons his hom lote and on of
the grat lots of medows with the severall devisons of
upland: upon condisons they bild ecth of them a
tenantable hous that is to say a hous upon ecth hom
lote and dwell with them four yers:

Att a meeting of the propriators of watterbury
march 21 1689: they agreed to be att the charge of the
transportation of m^r peecke above said and his famely
and cattell and goods to watterbury.

Att the same meeting they agreed the fens vewars
shod goe to vewing the fens this day: and leve it to
Ensigne Judd and Samuell hickox to send out the
hawards

At the same meeting the propriators made chois of
Samuell hickox Isaac brownson Obadiah richards to
tacke as prudent a care as they cane for to transporte
m^r pecke and famely and estate acording to the vote
above riten for the benifite of the Towne[1]

Att a meeting of the propriators of Waterbury
genewary: 26^d 1691 there was granted to corp^r Isaac

---

[1] Added at a later date:
    "Received to Record March 20, 1722.
    Recorded In first book, p. 9."

Brounson too acers on the north sid of his own four acer lot and to Run west till he meet with obadiah Richards to take the vacant land betwein his four acer lot and Obadiah Richards provided he live heir four yeirs.

Att the same meeting ther was granted to Corp John Welton six acers of land on the north sid of Isaac Brounsons four acer lot provided he Coinhabit four yeirs

Att the same meeting ther was granted to the eyers of Joseph Hikcox decesed three acers of land on the north sid of John Weltons six acers provided the said eyers or eyer com to live heir within four yeirs

At the same meetting the proprietors granted John Scovill four acres upon the litle brooke abuting north upon benjamin Jonses heirs land provided itt doe not pregudis high ways

Att a meetting of the propriators in Watterbury: March the 15 169½ there: was granted: to ecth propriator: inhabetant a devition of outland of ten acers to a hundred pound alotment and five acrs to a 50 pound alotmente and so proporsonable acording to mens alotments granted by the comite for the plas that is to say to thos that hould the poseson of the medow alotments by their own righte: each man to tacke itt up by suckseson after the lots are drawne the first too men to have two days liberty to tack his land: and bringe in his report to Ensign Judd who is to lay it out two them: and so to have on day two two men:

Att a meetinge of the propriators of Watterbury

January: 20 1692: that was graunted to John richards twenty acrs of upland provided hee tacke itt up in a hansom forme note enterfering upon the seqestered land nore pregedes high ways or former grants and dwell in the towne as a settled inhabetante six yers; and six acrs of medow or swampe that will macke medow: upon the same condisons that the twenty acrs above is:

Att the same meeting the propriators granted John richards a four acre lote upon the same condisions provided he relinqish his grant of a hous lote And give him till the last of March to tacke his land and itt is to be understood he may have his land for his four acre lot within the two mille bogy medows exeptede

Att a meeting of the propriators of Waterbury Jan 20 1692 they granted Danill porter the upland betwixt the comon fens and his land on the est side the river against stels medow and two extend southward too John newills aight acer lote & from that a west lyne to bound him upon the river

Att the same meting they granted Danill porter a pes of lande att the est end of his medow lote in hope medow buting him upon the cove not to pregedes high ways

Att the same meetting ther was granted John hopkins on acre and a half on the north side of his four acre lote provided it doe not prejedis high ways

Att the same meeting ther was granted to Daniell Worner six acers of lande south warde from the old town plat:

Att the same meeting ther was granted to thomas

Richason all the comon land one the west sid of his
fens against hancox medow and so to met with his est
stak

At the sam meting thear was granted to thomas
warner a peas of vaquent land one the west sid of the
pine hill and so to bute north on his one land and west
one the coufe

Att the sam meting ther was granted to Isaac
brounson and thomas Richason liberty to spring
out one the est side of ther foure acers lots so as to
run aperrerlal line from the south est corner of Richard
porters lot to the south est corner of thomas Richasons
lot not to pragedish hyways and foremer grants

Att the same meetinge the propriators granted John
Standly the coman land att the weste end of his land
att bucks medow and at the west end of Joseph hickox
ser lande and Isaac brownsons land and to extende
southward to tacke in the broocke that coms from
Isaacks yard so as itt be no pregedis to him: and to
extend to the tope of the mountain; or, so far as may
be most convenient for fensinge in the medow or a
paster itt not too pregedis high ways

Att the same meeting ther was granted John wilton
Junr the hous lotte formerly granted two John richards
which he relinqished on condisans itt doe not pregedis
high ways or former grants and dwell as a setteld in
habitant in the town sixe yers: and buld acording too
origanll articls

Att the sam meting thear was granted to abraham
andrus snr liberty if he relinquish the six acers granted
him one the hill at the twelf mill stak and the twell
acers of land at Turcy hill taken up as his medow
devistion: to tak it up somwhare one the south sid of
the bever pont brook abuting one his: last pich pro-

vided he hinder no former grant if theye pich on it between this and the first of maye

Att the same meting thear was granted to timothy Standly as part of his devishion a pes of land at the pin hill abuting one John warner south one a hyway est and one thomas warner north one the river west

Att the same meting thear was sequestered the grat brook from edmun scots lot down to samwell hickox ju^r lot for to build a fulling mill

Att the same meting thear was granted to roberd scot too acers and half of boggey medow ajining or buting one his former pich provided he coinhabit four yers.

Att the sam meting thear was granted to steven upson one acer of land one the north side of his four acer lot abuting on his lot

Att the same meting thear was granted to John welton and thomas judd the smith to met at John Welton's fens one the sid of the burnt hill

Att a meting of the proprietors in waterbury, Jenuary 20 1692 thear was granted to John Judd liberty to spring one the north sid of his lot agants leften Standlys fens up to the top of the hill for convenyans of fensing provided he coinhabit heare four years

Att the same meting thear was granted to Samll Hickox Snr. fuife acers of land one the north est end of his lot at woster swamp to run perrarlal with his lins from the swamp est ward

Att the same meting ther was granted to samll hickox jnr too acers of land one the sid of chesnut hill ner to his boggy medow convenyant for a yard as he can thar find

Att the sam meting thar granted to John welton snʳ too acers of land at his boggy medow one the south sid of wodbury rode part of itt on the west side the other part at the north end upon the brook

Att the same meting thear was granted to Danill porter a parsell of upland one the west sid of his land att the lower end of the long medow betwen his land and the eaight acer lot belonging to the eairs of John caring tons provided it dos not pragdish hyways

Att the sam meting thear was granted to Joseph Galord fuife acers of land on the west side of his boggy medow: one the top of the hill woodbury path running throw it

Att the sam meting the proprieters agred that Thos that hafe former grants hafe till the last of march to pich one ther plassis and bring in ther pich to the meserer then in being and if theye neglect theaye are not [to] hinder other grants

Att a meeting of ye propriators in Waterbury March 28: 1694/5 there was granted to Isaac brunson junr willyam hikcox and Thomas Richason junr twelve acers of land on ye south sid ye highway yt leads to farming town to but on ye high way and on ye south west coner of carrontons pond & run south ward and west ward till they have theyr twelve acers & devid it betwein them four acers a peic for a hous lot provided they build each of them a hous and inhabit according to origanal articles not to pregudis hiways or former grants

Att ye same meeting ther was granted John Richason four acers for a hog field one ye north sid ye higway yt leads to farmington & on ye east sid ye higway that Runs by Srg: Standlys lot in to ye wods north he not pregedising hiways nor former grants and fullfiling ye terms of origonal articles

att ye same meeting ther was granted to thomas hikcox four acers for a hous lot on ye west side carrontons brook one ye south sid ye highway yt leads to fermington not prejudising higways nor former grants he fullfilling ye terms of origanall articles

att ye same meeting there was granted to isriell Richason four acers for a hous lot if it be there to be had one ye north sid ye town between john judds four acer lot and daniell worners three acer lot he not prejudising higways nor former grants and full filling ye terms of origanell articcles

Att ye same meeting there was granted to John worner junr four acers one ye south sid ye higway yt leads to fermington on ye east sid carrintons brook to begin at ye brook and run east and south on them conditions yt it do not prejidis high ways nor former grants he fulfilling ye tarms of original articcles

Att ye same meeting they granted Joh Richards yt lot where his hous now stands as it lys buted south on Stephe ubson west on john hopkins & a great lot and thomas worner and north on ye path yt now leads to ye corn mill and liberty to Record it to him self and hyers

Att ye same meeting there was granted to Joseph gaylord junr four acers for a hous lot one ye great brook on ye north sid sam hikcox four acer lot to Run Cros ye brook and but on ye highways east and west he not prejedising higways nor former grants fullfilling ye tearms of origanal articcles

Att a meeting of ye propriators in Waterbury March

28 1694/5 benjamin barns was chosen as modirator to appoint meettings of ye propriaters and to leade in thos meetings

Att ye same meetting there was granted to Ephriam Warner from this day to begin his time for fullfilling of articcles for his hous lot and boggy meadow of seven acers upland and meadow formerly granted him not with standing any thing to ye contary he fullfiling origanal articcles

Att ye same meeting there was granted to David scott yt peic of land by macys lot on ye mill River betwein ye sawmill path and ye higway yt leads to farmington and to but on john macys lot and to ye botom of ye hill at bogs next yt sipach (see page) or bogs yt run from ye sawmill path to farmington Road not to take ye boogs he improving it within three yers not to prejedis higways or former grants

Att ye same meeting there was granted to joseph gaylard junr yt land betwein his lot and ye River at juds meadow on ye west sid ye River on ye hill aganst ye land yt belongs to ye heyrs of srg hikcox dect to Run a strat loy with his stack not prijedising higways

Att ye same meeting there was granted to isaac brunson junr and john Richason six acers on ye south west corner of ye long hill to be devided betwen them not prejedising highways nor former grants they improving of it and fullfill theyr conditions of theyr hous lots

Att ye same meeting ther was granted to wm hikcox john warner thomas hikcox thomas Richason jun twenty acers on ye East sid of ye long hill and on ye south sid benjamin barnses lot est end they to devid it equally betwein them not prejedising higways nor former grants they improving of it and fullfilling ye conditions of their hous lots

Att ye same meeting there was granted to Jonathan scott four acers of land at ye north end of Ensign Judds six acre lot he not prejedising higways nor former grants

Att ye same meeting there was granted to david Scott four acers for a pastor on ye north sid stp^h ubsons five acer lot on ye west sid of ye long hill he improving it with in four yers not prejedising higway nor former grants

Att the same meting it was granted to John Jud and John Richardson to take up that land which was formerly granted to them upon Steals brook in four parsels

At the same meating the proprieters granted to Ephrain warner and John welton twenty acres of Land at the est end of buks hill

At the Same meating the proprieters granted to Israel Richardson thre acres lying by the est side of his fathers lote aganst hancoks meadow

At the same meating the propriaters granted to thomas warner thre acers on the south est side of farmingtown rode runing south est to his one meadow from the hoge pound broke

At the Same meating the proprieters granted to Isac brown soun and william hecok twenty acres of land on the est side of hoge pound brook on bouth sids the rode

At the Same meating the proprieters granted to Joshua Peck a homelot wher he can find it betwen this time and the last of April next ensuing provided he bulde a house acording to original articles and dwel hear four yers   The above mentioned lote containing four acres

At the same meating the proprieters granted to
insine Thomas Jud a parsel of land on the est side of
hancoks brook buting west on the sade brook north on
John warner his land Sout on Thomas Jud junior
est on the above sade ensine his land

at a meting may the 30: 95: the propriators and town
granted to John Richards 3 acers of upland with half
the littel medo buting upon the north sid of the rode
to farming town: and so to meet with David Scot who
is to have the other half of the meddo joining to his
former grant: and the said Richards is to but south on
the rode and wes on the hil north at the saw mil path:
thes grants are upon the sam condisons as their grants
upon the grat brock:

at the sam meting the town granted 8 acers of boggy
meddo to John Richason and William Hickox: which
was for mer ly granted to John Brounson Jur liing
up the brok coming down to John Brownsons land
sener.   this grant is upon the sam condisons as there
other grants.

at the sam meting the town grants to Edman scot
a parsel of land laying within the comon fenc buting
east on the buring yard south on the grat lot north on
the fens west on the hig way:

at the sam meting there was granted to Daniel
Warner a pes of upland ley ing north to his three acer
lot est on timmothy stanly west on the hey way:

December 17, 1696 at a proprietors meting in Watterbury there was granted to John. Richason: John
Brounson Joseph Gaylord a parsel of land at Judds
meddo but ing south on Doct^r Porters meddo west on

the river and north on the rocks provided it dont prejdis hig ways nor former grants: provided they buld and cohabit according to articles

at the sam meting there was granted to John Hopkins John Richason Josep Gaylord John Brounson 14 acers of land leying eastward from ben ja min Jons lot at Juds meddo buting north at the hil and to run south.

at the sam meting ther was granted to Israel Richason a parcel of land liing north from steven upsuns lot on stels plain buting est on Abram Andrus and Phillup Juds lot north on John Hopkins and Mr. Peck, weste at the hed of the spring, provided he improve it within four yers

at the sam meting there was granted to John Brounson Stevn Welton Joseph Hickox John Gaylord 40 acers of land laying upon chesnut hil betwen hancox: brock and bucks meddo and 10 acers to thomus Richasun at the sam plas provided ther be ainof this is given upon conditions thay improve 3 or four acurs a pes with in eight yers

at the sam meting ther was granted to Israel Richasun: 4 acers betwen the pin hol and the comun fenc provided he improve it in eight yerss buting south on his fathers lot:

at the same meting ther was granted John Judd 6 acers leying north from the mil lot provided he improve 3 or four [acres] of it within 8 yers:

at a metting of ye propriaters in Waterbury Decembr 20d 1697   In order to ye seteling such yong men that desire to settell in ye town ye propriators grant to each one yt desires to settell for theyr incuragment for accomadation thirty acers of upland swamp and bogey meadow as a lot ment with a propriaty in ye commons according to theyr alotment with a hous lot and four acers for a pastor to be layd out to them by ye town measurer giving them four yers to build a tenantable hous not less than sixteen foots squar and he yt takes up a lot and is not in way of improvement and shall not build accordingly shall forfit his lot and what land has bin given to any yong man shall be accounted as part of his lot this act not to pregedes former grants nor higways this act to be in force for al such as live amongs us as they shall com of age and desire this privilidg and beacsepted by ye propriators but ye priviledg of acting in giveing away land we do not give them this alotment to be deemed a forty pound elotment in al Devitions and so to have theyr propriaty in ye commons and after 2 yers each a lot ment to be deemed as too pounds estate in ye bareing town charg: for 4 yers and after according as they improve according to law or apprisall of other lands in ye town and non to make sall of any but yt improved and· subdued but if any dye here his hirrs to poses his lands

at ye same meeting ye propriators gave ye doct portor liberty to tack his four acers in any part of ye wigwam swamp so yt he do Run acros ye swamp.

at ye same meeting they gave to abraham andruss jenor one acer and a half at judds meadow on ye East sd of ye brook yt runs in to benjamin barnses yard. . . .

att ye same meeting John Scovell was released from building on yt land joyning to john worners 3 acer lot:

att ye same meeting ther was granted to obadiah Richards juner three acers at ye hill one ye west sd

of bucks meadow yt he has al ready took up in part
he not to prejedis high ways

att ye same meeting ther was grated to Richards
four acers at bucks meadow at ye south west corner
of his Eyland at john brunsons land

att ye same meeting there was granted to stephen
ubson three acers of bogey meadow where ye grinlet
runs in to ye west bogey meadow on ye east sid of ye
long hill we say yt grinlet yt comes from ye east coner
of ye long hill

At a meeting of ye propriators in Waterbury March
26ᵈ 1699 Left judd Ensign Standly Deac Judd srg
bronson obadiah Richards sner John Wellton snr
and John hopkins was chosen a comity to view ye
pasage up Manhan meadow and to altor it to sum other
place according as they shall judg best for ye town and
moest for ye advantage of ye propriators

att ye same meeting Abraham andrews snr John
Worner ju and John hopkins was chosen a committy
to lay out a pasage to Judds: Meadows.

att ye same meeting ther was granted to benjamin
barns six acers of land at juds meadow at ye west
sid of ye spring against his yard he not to pregedis
highways nor former grants his land to be his according
to ye grant to isriell Richason in March: 10d: 1699.

Att ye same meeting Wm hikcox Joseph hikcox
Joseph gaylard John gaylard John brunson Isriell
Richason Stephen Wellton John Warner Thomas Richason were acsepted propriator inhabitanc according
to yt act Decembr 20ᵈ 1697:

Att ye same meeting there was granted to Ephriam
warnor five acers at ye north sd of john scovell at

hikcoxs mountayn on ye same condition yt ye young mens was

att a meeting of ye propriators in Waterbury May 15 1699 ye propriaters granted ye yong men liberty to take up theyr thirty acers in three places and if any have perticular grants of land to have them counted in ye 30 acers and not to hinder theyr pitches and he yt has had 3 pitches to have on more

at ye same meeting ther was granted Stephe ubson four acers with liberty to pitch on ye hill at ashe swamp

At a meeting of ye propriators in Waterbury May 15 1699 Ther was granted to Richard porter teen acers of upland where he can find it one ye same conditions ye yong mens not to pregedis former grants nor high wayes

att ye same meeting there was granted to daniell werner teen acers of upland at his Eyght acer lot at juds meadow on ye same conditiones ye yong mens was not to pregedis high wayes nor former grants

at ye same meeting there was granted to thomas warner teen acers of upland at his 3 acers at his bogey meadow over thre mill brook according as ye yong mens was not to pregedis high ways nor former grants

att ye same meeting there was granted to Stephen ubson six acers of up land at his hog feild at ye north sid of philips meadow on ye same conditions ye yong mens was not pregidising high wayes nor former grants

att ye same meeting there was granted to Edman Scott eyght acers of upland where he can find it on ye same conditions Richard porters was att ye same meeting there was granted to gorg Scott four acers for pastor near hikcox mountain

att ye same meeting there was granted to Joseph gaylord senr and Edman Scott four acers at juds meadow above where butlers hous was. for a pastor to be equally devided betwein them

at the same meeting ye propriators declare yt he which first brings in his pitch in wrighting to ye measurer not pitching where another has pitched befor shall give him title and not [be ac]counted a[s] prigedising former grants

att ye same meeting there was granted teen acers of upland where it can be found for a minister yt shall com to settle

att ye same meeting there was granted to John scovill four acers for a pastor on ye east sid of his mountain.

at a propryeter meten held at Warterbary may 15 1699   Thear was granted to gorg [Scott] ten acers of land one the hill whar Jonathan scot had ten acers of land granted to him one the west sid of the river aganst buks madow one sam condistions the young mens haufe theair land and not to pragadish hy ways and former gran[ts]

at the sam meting the propryeters granted to John scovll four acers of Land one the south end of his land one the aboufe said hill not to pragadish hi ways and former grants

at the sam meting thear was granted to efram warner ten acers of land one the aboufe said hill one the sam condistions the young men haufe theair 30 acers of Land and not to pragadish hy wais and former grants at the sam meting their was granted to David scot four acers of land one the west sid of his ten acers of land one the aboufe said hill one the aboufe said condistions and not to pragadish hy wais and foormer grants

att ye same meeting there was granted to Edman Scott a peic of land at juds meadows yt lyes betwein his eyght acer lot and his meadow lot

at ye same meeting there was granted to abraham andrews sener teen acers of land on ye hill aganst georges hors brook on ye same conditions yt ye yong mens was

att ye same meeting there was granted to John Judd teen acers on hikcox hill on ye same conditions ye yong mens was

att ye same meeting Robard Scott Thomas hikcox and Richard Wellton and John Richason was acsepted propriator inhabitants according to yt act in December ye 20 1697 John Richason relinquishes his 20 acers up steels brook for his being admited an inhabitant

att ye same meeting ther was granted to Deac Judd teen acers of upland where he can find it on ye sam conditions ye yong men had theyrs not to pregedish former grants or highwayes

att ye same meetin there was granted to John willton senor teen ac[res] of upland on ye same conditions ye yong mens was not to pregidis former grants nor high wayes:

att ye same meeting there was granted to obadiah Richards teen acres of upland on ye same conditions and not to prigedis former grants nor highe wayes

att ye same meeting there was granted to Thomas Judd jun teen a[cers] of upland on ye same conditions as deac Judds

4

att ye same meeting ther was granted doctor porter teen acres [of] upland where he can find it not to pregedis former grants

att ye same meeting thear was granted Joseph gaylard senr. teen acers of upland on ye same conditions deac Judds

att ye same meeting ther was granted to left Judd teen acers of upland on ye same conditions as deac judds

at ye sam met ing ther was grant ed to Isack Brounson ten a cars upon the for said con dis ons. at bucks hil north ward from Ephram worner and John Welton

At the sam met ing ther was Grant ed to John Hopkins ten a curs of upland on the sam condisons as Deacon Judds is

at the sam met ing is granted Tho Rich a sun sener ten acurs of upland as decon Juds is

at the sam meting ther was granted Ben Barns ten acurs of uplan at Brakeneck hil: join ing to the Worners upon the sam condisons as Decon Judds is

Att a meeting of ye propriators of Waterbury decembr: 23: 1700   Benjamin Wornor & obadiah Richards & Isaac Brunson junr ware exsepted propriatory inhabitanc according to yt act decembr ye 20: 1697:

Att ye same meeting there was granted to Doctor porter yt peic of Land at ye north end of his lot at juds meadow to com up to ye broock butiug east on ye hill west on ye River he not pregedising highways Joseph gaylard and John brunson and john Richason haveing Relinquished yt part of it yt was givn ym

att ye same meeting there was granted to Jonathan Scott and david scott four acers on ye west sid of the sd davids lot at hikcox mountain and one acer and half on ye East sd said lot they not pregedising high-ways

att ye same meeting there was granted to willyam hikcox John brunson John gaylard & Joseph hikcox teen acers at ye west sid of theyr land betwein hancox brook and bucks meadow they to Run so fare as to take ye spring:

att ye same meeting there was granted to Stephen Ubson a peice of land yt lyes partly betwein his peic of bogey meadow and ye path on ye East sd ye long hill which land Runs south west from sd meadow of Ubsons

att ye same meeting there was granted to John Worner four acers at ye west end of his moun-tain

att ye same meeting there was granted to En-sign timothy Standly teen acers of upland where he can find it not pregedising high ways nor former grants

att ye same meeting there was granted samuell standly teen acers of upland where he can find it not pregedising high ways nor former grants. he bringing in his pitch to ye town measure:

att ye same meeting there was granted to gorg Scott four acers at hikcox mountain a little westward of his own land not pregedising high ways being a pies yt he has already broak up summ of

att ye same meeting there was granted to Joseph gaylard sener four acers of land at juds meadow on ye south wesd sd ye brook yt comes in to edman scotts lot buting on ye three acres given to sd gaylord & scott & buting part on ye lot

att ye same meeting there was granted to edman

scott four or fuife acers at ye [   ] end of his land on
ye hill southward from bens meadow to run westward
to take ye spring

att ye same meeting there was granted to ye minister
ten acers of up land where he can find it not pregedising
high ways or former grants

att ye same meeting there was granted to John
Richards six acers on ye northwest sd of ye hill yt lys
nor west of crambury pond not pregedising highways
or former grants

att ye same meeting there was granted to benjamin
barns five acers at ash swamp tacking it on ye sids
joyning to his own land not pregedising highways
nor former grants

att ye same meeting there was granted to left thomas
judd six acers on ye easter sid of his land on ye hill or
mountain lot on ye west sd ye River

att ye same meeting there was granted to Stephen
Ubson and Joseph gaylord jur Eyght acers at ye
south west coner of sd gaylords land at ash swamp
not pregedising high wayes or former grants

att ye same meeting the propriators granted yt
thos yong men that build in ye town plat shall have
six acers for a pastor not takeing it where it would do
for a hous lot and they yt go out furder to build to
have four acers for a hous lot

att ye same meeting there was granted to thomas
warnor four acers on ye hill above john warners land
aganst doctor portors lot at juds meadow

att ye same meeting there was granted to obadiah
Richards senor one acer where his hous stands at his
mountain

att ye same meeting there was granted to Samuell
hikcox five acers joyning to his too acers on ye west

sd of chesnut hill not pregedising high wayes or former
grants

Att a meeting of ye propriators in watorbury March:
18: 1701 Ephariam worner abaraham andruss junr
and Willyam gaylard ware acsepted propriatory inhabitants according to yt act decembr the 20 1697
as to bachadelers accomidations

att the same meting the propryters gaufe Liberty
to efram warner to tak up his hoole devistion of land
or propritership one the north sid of bouks hill he
relinkqushing all his other grants exseping his home
lot and boggy madow it not pragedish ing hy wais and
fooremer grants

at the same meting the propriters gaufe liberty to
John Warner to take the remander of his propryty
ship along with efram one the north sid of bouks hill
he relinkquishing nine acers one the est sd of the long
hill it not pragydyshing hy wais and fooremer grants

att a meeting of ye propriators in waterbury decmbr: 23 1701 John Wornor taylor was excepted apro-
priator inhabitant on a bacheldrs a lot ment.—

att meeting of ye propriators in waterbury aprill:
6^d : 1702

ye propriators by voate agree that whosoever shall
have liberty to live or go on ye west sd ye fence or
great river within our bounds Shall submit to ye order
of ye propriators as if they lived on ye east sd ye com-
monfenc as to our agreement of fencing o[u]r meadows
yt by resin of them we be not under nesesity of fencing
on ye west sd our meadows but yt theyr creators be

pound fesent in any of our meadows and they oblidged
to keep theyr creators out of our feilds as if they ware
fenced round and he yt gos to live on ye west sid to
subscrib this act in testimony of his submiting to it and
he yt refuses to submit to this ordor not to be a lowed
to live on ye west sd

att meeting of ye propriators in waterbury aprill
ye 6: 1702:

Stephen Ubson had librty to Reliquish his twelve
acers at twelve milstak at to antock and to take it
by his own land at ash swamp

at ye same meeting thomas hikcox had librty to
relinquish his lot at wolf pit meadow and his lot aganst
mad meadow and to take it elswhere not pregedising
former grants: william gaylord at ye same time had
librty of removeing all his pitches and john gaylord
all his pitches but: at ash swamp and his pitch at ye
mountain up hancox brook on ye sam conditions
hikcoxs was and joseph gaylord junr had librty to
relinquish al his lot but abragadow & 4 acers at wst(?)
mountain: john richards had liberty to relinquish
15 acrs at hikcox mountain 3 acers at kenys lot on ye
sam conditions above metioned and to take ye bigest
half joyning to his own lad beyond wostor swamp and
ye rest ther a bouts

att ye same meeting srg brunson had teen acers of
upland given him at breakneck hill joyning to his own
land

att ye same meeting Richard porter had librty to
relinquish his 4 acers up handcox brook and his teen
acer deition and gave him six mor to take it up elswher
as it may not pregedising high ways and former grants

att ye same meeting daniell worner had librty to relinquish his 6 acers at ye southend ye old town plat and to take it at hog pound brook by thomas warners land not interfering with him

att ye same meeting ther was granted to srg brunson 4 acers and a half and joseph gaylard senor 4 acers and a half where brunsons hous stands at breakneck hill

att ye same meetting ye propriators gave Richard portor joseph gaylord [John] gaylord and william gaylord eyght acers apeic at ye plac they talck of go[ing] to live at on ye west sd provided they go and live there with theyr familyes

att ye same meeting ther was granted willyam hikcox eyght acers on ye west sid of his own land at ash swamp joyning to his own land

att ye same meeting there was granted to John Richards abraham andrus junr a swa[mp] betwein abrahams land and obadiah richards land to run twenty Rods down ye brook belo where ye path gos over and to run north ward to ye end of ther p[lowin]g land to devid betwein em

att ye same meeting there was granted to samuell hikcox at hikcox mountain to run from ye Southeast stack of his lot to ye southwest to take ye advantage of watering

att ye same meeting there was granted Ephriam wornor and John wornor Eyght acers apeic joyning to theyr own land at bucks hill for paustor not to pregedis high ways or formr grants

att ye same meeting there was granted to david scott and gorg scott Eyght acers of upland apeic at ye nor west sid of woster swamp of ye uper swamp

att ye same meeting ther was granted to stephen

ubson a peic of land betwein brunsons path yt gos
to his bogey meadow and ye path yt gos over ye
meadow to ye saw mill but ing on his own land in ye
bogey meadow

att ye same meeting there was granted to thomas
judd junr teen acers of land not pregedising highwas
and bringing in his pitch to ye measurer as others do

att ye same meeting there was granted to obadiah
richards jur five acers for a paustor betwein john
welltons land and sd richards es barn

att ye same meeting there was granted to benjamin
barns to spring from ye north coner of his lot next
isriell richason at ash swamp and run to ye brook and
so down to ye bogey meadow

att ye same meeting there was granted to deac thomas
judd eyght acers for apastor on ye west sd of yt land
yt was john wornors mountain

att ye same meeting there was granted to daniell
wornor too or three acers of land at juds meadow at
his eyght acer lot on ye south sd ye brook above where
ye old path went over ye brook

att a meeting of ye propriators in waterbury decembr 21 1702 they granted samll hikcox eyght acers of
land at Judds meadows aganst hikcox meadow where
he has set his hous to take it a bought his hous

att ye same meeting there was librty granted to
gorg scott to take six and twenty acers of land at
bucks hill or ther abought he relinquishing six and
twenty acers 12 acers above his 8 acer lot and 7 acers
westward of wostor swamp ye rest at hikcox mountain:

att ye same meeting there was granted to richard

portor too acers at his bogey meadow to take it partly
on booth sids his land

att ye same meeting there was granted to benjamin
wornor four acers at ye head of hog pound brook

att a meeting of ye propriators in waterbury february 22th: 170⅔

ye propriators declare yt ye propriators for ye first
purchasing of ye place and such as stand posesed of
alotments according to ye gran[d] commitys act with
stephen Ubson Richard portor and Jonathan Scott
whos alotments war excepted of ye commity as a
fifty pounds alotment apeic shall be acknowledged
propriatory inhabitants & to act in giveing a way lands
in sd propriatory ship and for ye futor no more to act
in ye propriators meeting then one for a singell alotment

at ye same meeting ye propriators took oft yt obligation of ye yong mens for subdueing and clearing as in
yt act decembr 20d 1697: and thos yt have now built ·
according to sd act to in habit five yeirs from this day
and then their lands be their own and others yt are
now acsepted on bacheldors accomadations and hereafter shall be excepted shall build according to said
act and inhabit five yeirs after they have build and
then their lands be their own:

att ye same meeting Stephen Ubson snor was chosen
modirator for ye propriators meetings

att ye same meeting there was granted to Joseph
gaylord snor six or seven acers of land on ye north
sd bucks hill on ye west sd ye cart path yt comes to
ye town and south sd ye path that gos in to the meadow
buting on john gaylords pitch on bucks hill

att ye same meeting joseph gaylord junr had librty of yt ground on which his hous stand and so to run from ye fore coners of his hous nect ye highway to ye coners of his hous lot—

at ye same meeting joseph gaylord junr had four acers buting on ye west end of his lot and runing west word he relinquishing his four acers given him at ash swamp for pastor not pregedising high ways

att ye same meeting Roberd Scott relinquished teen acers at long swamp west of john wornors mountain and ye propriators gave him leave to take sd teen acers on ye hill aganst scots and scovills land at juds meadows

att ye same meeting thomas hikcox and joseph hikcox relinquished their teen acers on ye hil est of wostor swamp yt was their fathers and had librty to take five acers apeic thomas to take his joyning to his own land at hikcox mountain and joseph to tak his joyning to his own land up hancox brook

at the same meting Insin Stanly had a libertey of changing a ten acor grant with Joseph Gaylard senor for his lot on the ould town-plot and said Gaylard to take up said ten acers at buks hil not to pregedis hig ways nor former grants

att the same meting the propriters gafe liberty for Decon Thomas Judd to re link yus his pich at the upper end of woster Swamp and tak it the west end or sid of the land he had of John warner gining to the land one scots mountain not pragedish[ing] hiwais [nor] former grants

at the sam meting the propriators gafe Jonathan Scot fuife acers of land at the north end of woster Swamp aboufe or next Jons lot est sd ye brook not to pragodish hi wais and former graunts

at a meeting of ye propriators in Waterbury March:
1^t 170¾

John Scovell was chosn to lay out or help Left
Timothy Standly his four acre lot

att ye same meeting ye propriators agreed yt y^e
fenc abought ye common feilds should be dun up by
ye = 10^d = of this moneth and ye meadows to be
cleard of ye cattell

att a meeting of ye propriators in waterbury decm^r
5–1704—John weellton senr srg isaac brunson & deak
udd was chosen a com⁻ity to veiu and measur from ye
lor end of ye long meadow to ye upr end of hancox
medow and so south to beakon brook and bring Report
of which may be most for ye advantag of ye propriator
to fenc Round from long meadow to ye upr end of
hancox meadow or south to beakon brook:

att ye same meeting srg Isacc brunson was chosen
modirator to lead in propriators meetings

att a meeting of ye propriators in waterbury decembr
ye 12 = 1704 and for a conclution in refirinc to a way
of fencing ye com⁻ on feilds ye voat first pased to see
if they would fenc southword from ye ould fenc to
beakin brook on ye east sd ye River and yt to be
counted sofisiant for ye seac[uring] ye feilds and it was
voated in ye negative: they yt voted in ye afirmative
in this voat was John hopkins Left Timothy stanly
jeremiah Peck doct portor Edman Scott

They yt votid in ye negetive: deak judd srg isaac
brunson joseph gaylord jur Stephen ubson snr john
scovell Tho Judd jur john Richards Thomas hikcox
isaac brunson jur Thomas Wornor gorg scott john
judd Thomas Richason

at ye same meeting

in ye second plac ye vote pased to fenc from ye
east end of ye mountain aganst moun taylor on
ye west sd ye River and so to ye falls in ye
River at ye lor end of ye long meadow and to make
ye fenc good and substachall aganst al ordrly horses
and cattell and sufficiant aganst too yeir olds and ye
fenc to be vewed by ye fenc vewers—they yt voated in
ye afirmitive of this voat deak judd srg brunson Tho
judd jur stephen ubson john scovell William hikcox
Thomas hikcox isaac brunson jun^r gorg scott john
judd jonathn scott john brunsoon Thomas Wornor.

att ye same meeting deak Tho⁻ judd Left Timothy
Stanly Jo^n hopkins sen^r benjamin barns sen^r & Tho⁻
judd jun^r Was Chosen a Com⁻ty to modell ye land in
sd feild and proportion ye fenc of sd feild to each man
according to his propriaty & lay out to each man his
part ye lands on which ye fenc is to be laid is all yt
is fit for plowing or moing in sd feild having Respect
to ye fenc alredy layd out each man to keep his fenc
alredy layd out to him and there being much land
spoyled with ye flood ye oners of such land to be considered and abated in this division yt ye whol Rang
of fenc of sd feild may be equally proportioned to
each propriator according to his benifit of lands in sd
feild as neer as they can

att a meeting of ye propriators in watorbury decm^r:
12 = 1704

they granted liberty to any yt see caus to inclos
in prticulor in sd feild for wheet or other corn

att ye same meeting ye propriators by voate agreed
yt he yt lefs opin ye com⁻on gatess or bers in ye com⁻on
feild should pay al ye damag yt is dun thereby and yt
no man shal stak horses in ye moing land in said feild

or baight cattell after ye first of aprill till com⁻ing time
except they are at work by ym and ye fences of sd
feild to be keept up al ye yeir and hogs pound fesiant
al ye yeir

att a meeting of ye propriators in Waterbury march
ye 5ᵗʰ 170⁴/₅

ye propriators by voat agreed yt ye fenc already
layd out on ye east sid for ye feilds shall be erected
according to law and an addition at the south end to
keep out horses and cattell being dun by ye direction
of ye modirator so fare as may be needfull and for ye
best advantage of ye feilds our feilds shall be accounted
pound fesiant for our cretors this yeire

att ye same meeting they ordored ye com⁻ty chosen
decmbr ye = 12 = 1704 to modall ye land in ye feild
and lay out ye fenc on ye west sid to sd feild go on with
theyr worck forthwith

att ye same meeting ye propriators agreed to leave
a mile at ye north end of ye loyn wher they begin to
measure on ye west sid where they intend to set ye
fenc to be dun by ye propriators in a genarall way
to be layd on ye land yet undevided as it shall be
taken up

att ye same meeting the propriators agreed to com
to a lot for ye fenc on ye west sid ye River and to begin
to lay out at ye loer end of ye long meadow wher sd
fenc is to com to ye River

att ye same meeting ye propriators gave benjamin
barns senor a little peic on ye coner of ye hill betwein
stephen ubsons plain & his own on steels plain and his
own lot on steels brook a straight loyn with his own land

att ye same meeting ye propriators gave juds meadow men leave to set up a pound for ymselves on their
own charg for impounding their own cattell and such

as are left out in ye feild when men are at worck with
them there

att a meeting of ye propriators in waterbury aprill
ye 9: 1705 ye propriators agree yt ye fenc belonging
to ye feild now to be fenct from ye uper end of hancox
meadow to ye loer end of long meadow shall be as
followeth yt ye whole Rang of fenc quit Round sd
feild shall be equally divided on ye acer alike of all
sorts of land with in sd feild booth of plowing moing
upland and pauster yt is allready layd out or given to
any man and each man to maintain his fenc so layd
out to them but ye fenc already layd on ye east sd
to remain and belong to them yt it belongs to not to
Remove them but to be counted as part of their divition
as fare as it will go ye former act by this made void in
exsempting pastor lands considring waste lands and
modalising

this voat was full but four or 5 acted aganst it and
doctor portor one of them did protest aganst it

att ye same meeting aprill ye 9th 1705 ye propriators
gave John Scovell five acers of upland joyning to ye
west end of his three acer lot and so runing to wards
ye meadow and a little pece of land at ye west end of
his hous lot esteimed abough a Rood he not to pregedis
high ways nor former grants

att ye same meeting ye proprietors gave isaac brunson jur and john brunson twelve acers of land on ye
south sd woodbury Road joyning joyning to breakneck hill provided they build on it

att ye same meeting there was granted to john
Richard five acers att ye brok west wher ye fenc is to
go at ye south sid his eyght acer lot over ye River
provided he build on it in three yeirs

att a meeting of ye propriators in Waterbury decemr -11-1705 by vote they agreed yt ye fenc layd out on ye west sd ye river for fencing in ye feilds shall be dun according to their act by ye last of aprill next:

att ye same meeting ye propriators gave ye men that have land up ye River liberty to but their fenc for secureing their land on ye com⁻ fence on ye west sd ye river and they haveing fenced from yt for their security non in ye town to turn cattell into their fields

att ye same meeting they granted richard wellton five acers at ash swamp buting on john gaylord south on john wornor east ye highway west not to pregedis high ways

att ye same meeting they gave Richord Wellto a peic of land att bucks hill buting on isriell pitch north west on a brook yt runs out at ye westend of bucks hill; on ye south on ye ston pit est on ye brook yt runs out ye great bogey meadow not to pregedis high [ways] nor former grants nor to hinder any fetching ston or timber [from] sd land as long as it lys unfenced

att ye same meeting there was granted to John hopkins senor six or seven acers of land joyning to his lot at juds meadows he not to pregedis high ways or former grants nor com over ye brook northward

att ye same meeting there was granted to daniell wornor a peic of land at juds meadow on ye hill at ye north end yt he had of john worner extending north to ye end of ye hill at ye hollow where his cart path gos up

att ye same meeting there was granted to ephriam wornor and Richard Wellton teen acers apeic of land up hancox brook if it be there to be had after ye men yt have land there have laid it out they not to pregedis high ways att ye same meeting there was granted to Sam^{ll} hikcox a peic of land at juds medow to extend north as fare as his own land sout to ye brook yt runs by his hous west on daniell wornor and ye rocks east

att ye same meeting left Tim Stanly deak judd was chosen commity to lay out what highways and pasages are needfull for ye town

att a meeting of ye propriators in Waterbury genuary-7th-170⁵/₆

it being voated whether ye propriators would devide theyr commons according to purchas or no ye voat past full in ye negetive yt they could not devid their commons but in ye second voat yt they would give away their land to particulor men as they see caus or as they shall judg men have need of it

att ye same meeting ye propriators voated to take ye forfituer of all ye lands yt was given to Joseph galard jur Joseph hikcox abraham andrus jur and ben⁻ wornor yt they cant hold by ye records

att ye same meeting there was grated to Joseph gaylord senr teen acers of land at ye west end bucks hill to begin at ye muddy gutter and spring east ward

att ye same meeting there was granted to Richard portor teen acers of land at his eyland south end betwen ye bogey meadow and mill river

att ye same meeting there was granted to Ephriam wornor five acers in ye swamp at ye north end of isriells feild at bucks hill

att ye same meeting ben⁻ barns jur Stephen Ubson jur was axcepted propriators on bacheldors accommidation according to ye propriators act

att ye same meeting there was granted to John

wellton jun four or five acers at ye south east end ye
long swamp

att ye same meeting there was granted to John gaylord teen acers on hancox brook not pregedising former
grants or high ways joyning to Ephriam warner and
Richard wellton

att ye same meeting there was granted to Jonathan
Scott five acers to joyn to his lot att ye north end of
woster swamp

att ye same meeting there was granted to abraham
andrus sener liberty to record his teen acers layd out to
him on bever pond hill

att ye same meeting there was granted to deak
Tho⁻s judd Six or seven acers of land south sd woodbury Road and sled hall brook not pregedising former
grants or high ways

att ye same meeting there was granted to John
hopkins teen acers of land att woster swamp at ye
south west end his own lot not to pregedis highways

att ye same meeting there was granted thomas
warner too acers on ye south sid yt was ben warners
at hog pound brook

att ye same meeting Left Timothy stanly was chosen
modirator

att ye same meeting there was granted to sam¹
hikcox all yt land yt lys betwen ye too brooks south
of his hous at juds meadow to run as ye brook runs
and from ye meadow and to Rocks at ye south east
coner of his tother grant: he haveing relinquished
ye pin swamp at mil river theree acers south of goldens
meadow and five acers on ye sd of chesnut hill

att ye same meeting there was granted to Left
Timothy Stanly twenty acers of land at E scotts 8
acer lot buting on his own land west or nor west

att ye same meeting there was granted to David Scott teen acers at a brook yt runs in at ye uper end of ye loer swamp at woster to spring west and south

att ye same meeting there was granted to stephen ubson seven or eyght acers of bogey meadow in a litle meadow south west of hop brook not pregedising former grants

at ye same meeting Thomas wellton gorg wellton and Joseph brunson was excepted proprietors on bacheldors accommodations according to ye propriators act

at ye same meeting of ye propriators Jan 7: 170⁵/₆ there was granted to edman scott seven acers a long with Stephen ubson near hop swamp if it be there to be had not pregedising former grants

att ye same meeting there was granted to gorg scott five acers of land at ye east end his lot at woster swamp not to pregedis high ways [or] former grants

att ye same meeting ther was granted to john richason five acers at woster swamp at ye west end of his fathers lot not to pregedis high ways or former grants to run a parell loyn with sd lot

att ye same meeting there was granted to jeremiah peck five or six acers of bogey meadow at ye south west sd his own land at his mountain joyning to yt he had of gorg scott

att a meeting of ye propriators in Waterbury: may: 3ᵈ 1706

they not haveing erected the common fenc on ye west sd ye fields by ye last of aprill past by voat [to] lengthen out ye time to ye last of this may and then to be dun according [to] their agrements for fencings att ye same meeting Stephen hikcox was admited a propriator on bacheldors accommondations according to ye act decm = 20th 1697 =

att ye same meeting stephen Wellton had liberty to relinquish twelve acers on good hill beyond woster swamp and to take it above bens meadow at ye south sd spruss brook on ye east sd long bogey meadow brook

att ye same meeting they gave thomas hikcox had five acers given him on ye hill aganst ye pasnag land up steels brook to tak fenc for it according to proprietors act

att a meeting of the propryters desember 17 1706 it was agred upon by vote that the fens from the est end of the mounttan aganst mount taller one west sid of the River and so to the fals in the river at the louer end of the long meadow [   ] and to mak the fens good and substanshel acording to [   ] and the land to be modell lised in said field and proportion the fens of said feild to ech man according to his propryety us to lay out to ech man his part—the lands on which the fens is to be laid is all that is fit for plowing or moing in said feild haufing respct to the fens alredy Laid out ech man to keep his fencs already laid out to him on the est sid and thear being much land spoiled by the flud the own ers of such land to be considered and abatted in this devistion that the whole Rang of fens of said feild may be equally proportioned to ech propryeter according to his benyfitt of Lands in said feld as ner as they can

att a meeting of ye propriators in Waterbury decm 24 = 1706 ye propriators order each propriator in complianc of ye above ritten act ye 17th of this instant according to sd act to bring in ye account of their land in sd field to ye comity yt should be chosen to model sd lands & to proportion sd fenc accord ing to sd act

att ye same meeting Thomas judd ju^r John hopkins sen^r & deak judd were chosen for a commity to model ye land in sd feild and devid ye fenc according to sd act =

Stephen ubson senr John wellton senr & abraham andruss for a com⁻ty according to sd act to modle ye lands of ye above sd com⁻ty

att a meeting of ye propriators in Waterbury decem 24 1706

There haveing bin dificulty in refirenc to ye fenc on ye west sd ye River ye propriators for to attain a peicable proceding haveing agreed to modle ye land in sd feild as may be seen by their act and now do com to a new lot agree by voate yt if by a new lot any man yt haveing fenct be removed he yt falls to have his fenc shall be Responcable to him yt mad ye fenc by their agreement and if they cannot agree to be dissided by too indifirent men by them chosen yt are concerned ye fenc to Rang in ye loyn already stacked out with liberty to take in Richard porters land above bens meadow if it may be dun without disadvantage

⌊ abraham andrs alone protested aganst it ye voat cleere. ⌋

att ye same meeting the propriators agreed by voat yt ye fenc to be loted out on ye west sd should be layd out no furder than it was before to com there or there abought leiveing ye rest according to former act to be dun by ye propriators in a generall way

att ye same meeting Sam^{ll} hikcox relinquished 18 acers att Scotts mountain westerly of thomas hikcox

and Joseph lewis had liberty to take it up at juds
meadows joyning to his own land not pregedising highways or former grants

and sam[ll] hikcox Relinquished 5 acers of swamp
at sd mountain lying next to judds land and gave him
leave to take it at juds meadows joyning to his own
land at juds meadow

att the sam meting the propriters granted by vote
that dan[ll] warner relinquishing seaven acurs of land at
warners good hill and six acurs at hog pound broak
and tak up seaven acurs betwien the brocks cald
danell warners broks and six acurs gining to his one
land at judds medows it not pragadishing hy wais and
fooremer grants

ye lot for ye fenc on ye west sd ye River as it fell
decem[r] 24th = 1706 = to begin at ye falls at ye long
m[eadow]

mr southmaid	12	abraham andruss	45
deak judd	43	john Richason	—11
john hopkins &	39	samll Stanly	–19
mil land			
john welton	31	widow joanes	–1
Left Tim Stanly	–4	m[r] bull — —	30
Stephen ubson	47	john warner	–50
Tho judd ju[r]	23	joseph gaylord	–08
jonathan Scott	18	widow brunson	= 17
Thom[s] Richason	–5	doctr porter	–26
Edman Scott	28	isaac brunson jr	–2
gorg Scott	—29	wid andruss	–25
jerem Peck	37	john brunson	:7:
John judd	— 3	Richard porter	32
Stephen Hikcox	20	pasnag	16
serg brunson	—48	scoall land	14

danniell warner	33	Tho-s warner	22
john scovell	—10	stephen welton	27
ben hikcox	−41	Tho porter	−9
ben judd	−42	Thos nuell	21
philip judd	−15	john carrinton	−6
John Richard	−40	obadiah Richards	24
Ebenzr hikcox	−49	joseph hikcox	−13
Willm hikcox	−44	joseph lewis	34
ben barns	−36	David scott	38
Thom^s hikcox	−46	Robert scott	35

y^e Totall of y^e Rods of ofenc

y^e east sd	1754	it exte [torn]
y^e west sd	1536	north [torn]
		division

att a meeting of ye propriators in Waterbury genuery ye = 7 = 170$\frac{6}{7}$ ye propriators agree yt ye fenc Round their field and gates shall be kept up all ye yeir and hogs pound fesiant all ye yeir and when sd field shall be opened to turn in cattell it shall be but one moneth and then ye cattle kept out and pounded as in ye sum⁻er and yt men shall turn into sd feild according to their intrest in it and no man to baight or stake in sd field at no time but on his own land and takeing care of them and all that brake this order to have their cattle pounded or delt with as trespasers

at a meeting of the propriters march 5 1711 It was grd on by vote the *moneth* in the aboufe record is intended for *munthe* and with that amendation the act to stand yearly till the propriters se cause to alter it

att a meeting of ye propriators in Waterbury genuery = 7: 170$\frac{6}{7}$ the propraters by vote admitted mosis

brunson to be a proper inhabitant and grantted him
a bagelders acomandation as other young men

at the same meting the propriters admitted nathanill
richason to be a propritor inhabitant and granted him
a bagilldors a coming dation as other young men

at the same meting thar was granted to thomas
warner seaven acers of land one warners good hill the
land thatt danill warner Relinquished

at the same metting Decon Thomas Judd is chosen
moderater for tim to com.

att a meting of the propriters may 12th 1707 it was
agred upon by vott that thos men at the south end
of the est sid fens that is agred upon too [be] Remoufed
shal be remofed by the oners of the fens and the propriters are to gife them for their remoufing it ten
pens a rod in good pay to the satisfaction of the thos
men that remofe ther fens

att the sam meting the propriters agre by vote that
the fens one the west sid the River shal be don by the
last day of June next and afer that the fens vewers are
to vew al the fens laid out for to secur sad feild and to
fine it as the law dyrects and the medows to be pound
fesent untill the last of october next or open soner if
the propriters se cas

att the sam meting it was agred that the fens one
the west sd the river shal be don for this yere only
against catell and not aginst hogs and the fens vewers
to it vew as such

at the sam metting the propriters gaufe to ^r_m Jhn
south maid fourscore acars of land on the south sid
of the Rock cald mount taller one the top of the hill
wher we get rals as part of his propryty in the com-
muns and do tak of the intailment of fensing in the

comon lin for said land it not to pragodis hi wais and
former grants the town hafing liberty to fetch timber
and stones they shuting up bars as there shall be need

at the sam meting the propriters gafe to david scot
ten acers of land on the west sd the river agst the uper
end of handkox medow on the hill west from william
hickox land on this condistion he making fens in the
common line as the Rest of we do for our land within
within said fens for all that is fit for moeing or plowing

A propriators meting held at Wtrbury decemb the
8 1707 it was voaeted by the properators that nither
hors nor cattel shold be baited or staked within the
feeld from the fifteenth of april until the medows are
clear furder it was voted by the propriators that each
propriator shold put in cretures according to ther
propotion of fence

at the sam meting it was furder voted that the fenc
on the west side of the meddow shold be don up by the
last of March next

At the same meting the propriators admitted john
barns and thomas Brounson to be inhabitance

at the same meting the propriators gave jonthan
scott a pece of land liing on the east end of his lot at
hecox meddow in case he maks fens proposhunal to one
acer in the comon line

att a meting of the propriters in Waterbury genyuary 5th 170⅞ it was agrd upon by vott to take
the forfillenr of all the land given on condistion to
thos men gon out of town that can nott hold them
by record: in not fulfilling the condition given upon

att the same meeting Thomas Richards and danill
porter jur were admittd propriter in habitans and to

have a bagelders acomindation acording to the grantt
in 1697 and the grant 170$\frac{2}{3}$

att a metting of the propriters genyuary $^{th}_{5}$ 170$\frac{8}{9}$
It was agred upon by vott to give doctr porter ten
acers of land one the plan south of smug swamp brook
between that swamp and the spakticell pon one the
acountt of a medow lot in the last devistion of
meadow up the river by lot belonging to Joseph
hickox eairs

att the same meting ther was given to moses brunson
a pes of land at his bogey medow buting one his one
land est north west and one Richard porter south one
the sam condistion the young men had thers

att the sam meting thear was given to gorg scot and
david scot a forty pound proprity in the undevided
lands when they come to be devided and to Jhon welton
jur the same privelig:

att the sam meting thear was given to decon Thomas
Judd a peas of land buting est on comon fents north
one the aiers of obediah richards three acer lott and
south and west one the eaight acer lot originally
belonging to philip Judd eairs now decon Judds eaight
acer lott

att the sam meting the propriters gave william
hickox thre roods or an acer of land one the south end
of his land one the hill one the west of hickox land on
the west sd the river in lew of a pes of land the common
fens cuts of from his land on said hill not to pragedis
hi wais

att the same meting ther was given to John scovill
six acers of land one the west sid his one land and
Joseph gallerds land at a plas cald sovells iland one thes
condistions it do not pragadis hiwais and former grants

and he fens for as much as is fit for plowing and moing
as they do for medow land and as part of his devistion
in comon field

att the sam meting thear was given to Jhn hopkins
snr twenty acers of land one the est sid of the mad
river one a run that fals in on the est sid said rivr
at the turn of it aganst the north end of the sawmill
plain it not to pragodis hiwas and former grants

at the sam metting granted to Tho Richasun four
acers of upland Joyning est ward to his mountain lot
not to prejudis high ways:

at the sam meting granted to John Brounson thre
or four acers of land west from the north end of Hicox
eight acer lot south from Abraham Andrus eight acer
lot not to pregadis highway and to bar fens a cord in
to the land

at the sam meting granted to John Judd too acers
of land upon the hil este from Thomus Judds lot at
hankox meddo he to fens acording to the land

at a meeting of ye propriators in waterbury genuary
ye 6th = 170$\frac{7}{8}$

ye propriators sequestered for ye use of ye town
too miles from ye going down of ye hill beyond Thomas
hikcox hous east and then from yt too miles north and
too miles south and then to Run at each end west
to ye como—n fence

att the sam meting it was agred upon by vott to
have a devistion of upland and meadow to be dcvided
as foluwes tht is to say every propritar that has one
hundred pound proprity to have fifty acers of land and
so mor acording to theair proprity and thos men from
upward of forty pound to a hundred pounds proprity
to have forty-five acurs a peace and thos men that are

forty pounds proprity and so under to have therty
acurs apese and to draw lots for said devistion

att a meeting of ye propriators in waterbury febru
$^{th}_{19}$-170$\frac{7}{8}$ by voutt they agreed to cancle ye words: (*so
under*) in ye second loyn from ye. botom of ye act
above this

att ye same meeting they granted ebenezer wornor
to take his part in ye divition above agreed on according to his interest in his fathers lot in ye bogey meadow
yt lys north west of serg brunsons meadow westward
of break neck hill

att ye same meeting ye propriators by voate agreed
yᵗ ye above sd devetion shall be taken: up as follows
yᵗ is to say [each] particular lot or propriatie in one
peice and after ye lot is drawn in any of ye undevided
lands except ye sequestered lands

att ye same meeting ye propriators agreed to burn
about ye com⁻ fenc northward from ye town ye first
monday in march and on ye west sd ye afternoon of sd
day and ye next day south from ye town but if ye
wether dont suite then ye next sutible season ye townsmen causing ye drum to be beat ye night befor to give
warning

Att a meeting of ye propriators in waterbury apr^l
$^{th}_{12}$-1708

ye proprietors of ye feild by a magor voate agree yᵗ
ye fenc Round sd feild shall be dun according to law =
on ye east sd frothwith but it being a busey time ye
west sd being dun substansiall aganst all sorts of cattell
but sheep and hogs ye fenc vewers are not oblidged this
yeir to vewe it but as such and ye owners of ye fenc
to do up ye west sd by ye last of this aprill

att ye same meeting ye proptors by a mager voate agree to chose a commity who in seven moneths shall by measureing all ye land in sd feild to be fenct for to proportion sd fenc Round sd feild according to mens interst and benifit in sd feild not to move any from their lot where their fenc now lyes but to Regulate mistackes if any be and if any are over charged to have it taken off and they yt want to have it but if any have not enough fenc and it be not in ye loyn staked out to take it by succession at ye north end ye southward man to be first   so sucsesively   Sam^{ll} Stanly

Att a meeting of the propriters in Waterbury october 11 1708

for a commity to masur the land in the said feild for which men are to fenc for and modellys acording to mens intrest and benyfit in said field to be don within or aboutt a month from the date her of ware abraham andrus snr John hopkins John Judd and Decon Judd

Att the sam meeting the propriters gave to Stevn upson [a piece] of land west of his six acer lot to but him one the comon fenes west of his said lott

Att a meting of the propriters in waterbury march 14 1709

it was agred upon by a mager vote to chous a commity who forth with shall by masuring all the land in said feild to be fensd for to proportion said fens Round said feild acording to mans Intrest and benyfit in said feild not to moufe any from thier lot whear their fens now lieth but to ragolat misstaks if any be

for a comity to do said work of masuring and proportioning said land and fens ther was chosen stevn upson snr John Scoill and thomas Judd smith

at the sam meting it was agrd on by vot to burn about
the fenses one the west sd on the 21 march and 22
day one the est sid if it be a good day if not the next
good day to be warned by the beat of the drum ovr
night and the fens one the est sid the gaps stopd and
gats shut forth with and the west sd quickly aftr it is
burnt about

at a meting of the propriters march 14 1709 it was
agred upon by vote for this year a good three raled
fens four foots hig well erected or equivilent to it
Shall [be] demed sofistient: one the west sid the river

at a meting of the propriters in Waterbury March
31 1709 by a mager vott it was agred to cal the fens
cros the mad river in the comon line seaven Rod
att the same meting the propriters agre by vott by
the comity to mesur the fens one the est sd the comon
feild   ech mans pies by it self
att the sam meting the propriters by a unannymus
vote agree to Remoufe the comon fens from the west
sd of thomas Richasons lott agnst the loer end of
hand kox medow to the est sid of said lot so thens a
strat line as may be to the the said comon fens aganst
hickoxs hools and all the land taken in to the comon
feild by said remoufe to be fensed for as the rest of
said feild is acording to the judgmet of the comity

an account of the number of the acers of land ech man has to fens for in the gennerall feild as it was meesured by us	waterbury april 18 1709 an account of the number of rods of fens men have one est and west sd for said land

Thomas Judd |
stevn upson | comity in March
john scovell | 1709

	A R.r.ft	East r.	ft	in		west r	ft
1 widow Jons	11 0 2	52	2	6	+	5	5
2 Isaac brunson							
3 John Judd	25 0 4	56	7	6	—	70	0
4 Lft Tim Stanly	38 1 4	66	0	10	—	125	7
5 Tho Richason	13 0 3 4	30	0	8	—	35	0
6 Jhn Carington	05 0 3 8	no fenc on ye west sd					
7 John brunson	09 1 1 1	39	7	6	—	11	7 6
8 Joseph gallurd	04 0 0	60	0	0	—	20	4
9 tho porter	05 1 0	19	14	0	—	08	0
10 abraham andrus	27 0 0	48	13	0	—	86	08
11 John Richason	07 0 0	12	06	0	—	23	03
12 Mr Southmaid	21 0 1	70	16	0	—	35	00
Scool land	07 0	39	02	6	—	38	01
philip Judd	15 1	53	08	0	—	39	
pesonage	18 1	44	01	06	—	non on ye west sd	
widow brunson	08 1	16	07	00	—	21	01
jonath scott	07 1						
Saml stanly	29 0	57	01	0	—	89	01
Tho nuell	01 1	00	00	0	—	07	08
Tho warnor	06 0 1	no fenc on west sd					
Tho Judd jr	23 0 1	92	2		—	23	14
obadi richards	10 0	42	9		—	07	
widow andrus	14 1 1	24	7		—	29	
doct portor	26 1	62	0		—	69	1
Step n welton	11 1 8	08	4		—	49	
Edman Scott	19 1 1	47	14		—	51	0
gorg Scott	16 1 1	63	0		—	22	11
mr. bull	04 0 1	00	0		—	21	
Jn welton	18 1 1	47	9		—	48	
Rich porter	10 0 1	30	12		—	20	
Danll warner	02 0 0	16	0		—	00	a
Ben barns	21 1 0	52	5		—	55	8
Jer peck	30 0 0	83	0		—	67	0
David scott	11 1 0	32	13		—	24	11
Jon hopkins	22 0 0	59	03		—	50	13
Mill land	19 1 0	00	00		—	97	08
John Richards	18 1 0	14	08		—	79	00
ben hikcox							
ben judd							
deac Judd	47 1 0	99	05		—	138	8

	A R. r.	East r.	ft		r	west ft
wm hikcox	21 0 1	34	8	—	44	14
						& 25
John scovill	21 1 1	46	15	—	61	12
						& 25
Tho hikcox	19 1 0	37	10	—	34	05
Stephen ubson	24 1 1	67	06	—	57	00
serg brunson	17 1 0	73	14	—	13	10
nezer hikcox	00 1 1					
John warner	01 0 0	3	0	—	02	0
Thos welton	1 0 1	6	4			

A Meeting of the proprietors. March 6th 1709–10
March 6th 1709–10 the proprietors Agreed by vote
that the beating the Drum through the town over night
shall be worning that the fence on the west side is to be
burnt About the next day and on the East side ye day
following

March 6th 1709–10 the proprietors granted to
Samuel Hikcox the Liberty of that Stream Called
daniel worners Brock. from the East Side of the going
over the Sd Brook. Any place for Conveniency of
Daming So Long as he Shall maintain A fulling mill
and Conveniency of Land to pass and dry Cloth.
not pregudicing Highways or former grants.
    att the sam meting the propriters by vott agre to
go on with the lot gred on at a meting in jenyuery 6
170⅞ and in order thar to mak chous of Jhn hopkins
Saml Stadly to fit a lot and one monday next 1710 to
met at twelf a klok then to draw the lot
    att the same meting the propriters by voate meak
chos of John hopkins Samll Standly Thomas Judd as a
commity to tak an acountt of the charg of mesuring
fens and land and remoufing fencs in the comon feild

and mak a rat one the land in said feild and so by the
acur to pay said charg

att a meting of the propriters in waterbury march
13 1710

the propriters by a mager vott gave nathanill Richason four scor acurs of land on the north sid the rood
to Wodbury up the grat brok est from break nek hill
to be taken in good forme in one peis one thees condistion that he tak it as his hole proprity as a bachelders acomydation and coinhabit ten years in the town
in a seteled way and bild a tenitabel hous acording to
originell artyculs in five yers and coinhabit 5 yers
after bulding his hous but if he leve the town within
said 5 yers the land return to the proprietors extrordi-
narys exsepted

leften timothy standly Edman Scott Jeremyah
Peack protested against the vote on the other sid. of
nathanll richason

att a meting of the propriters march 13 1710 the
propriters by vott gave Joseph luis 5 acurs of land by
his own at judds madows on the condistion he relinkquis
a peic of boggy madow of 4 or 5 acurs west of the north
end of the long hill formerly given to him

att the same meting the propriters by vott gave
mr Sothmaid four scor acurs of land as far from the
town as mount tallur he taking it in one pes in a good
form he Re link quishing the four scor acurs given him
at the said mount taler formerly given him

att the sam meting the propriters gave edman scot
leve to Record the pes of upland for his one at the est
end of his lot in handkox madow: upon condistions he
maintan the fens layed out to said land

march 13 1710 an a count of the propriators propriaty [in] order to a division of upland as was agred
on Jan: 6: [170⁷/₈]

Mr Southmaid—150
Deac Tho: Judd—100
John Scovil
Ben Jons:
John Warner
tho porter:
Jonathan Scott
John Richason
Tho Hancox
Tho Richason
John Brounson
Tho Judd
Dannil Warner
Obadiah Richards
Willim Judd
Wil Hickox:
Samwel Hickox: Sr
Ben Barns:
John Richason:
Steven Upson sr
Stephen Upson jr
Richard Porter:
Doctor Portor:
Abram Andrus cop
Timmothy Stanly
John Carington:
Gorg: Scott
David Scott

John Judd
Isack Brounson sr
Sam Standly
John Stanly
John Neuel
Josep Gayler sr
Stephen Welton
Tho Hikcox:
John Brounson
Israel Richason:
Jerymiah Peck
Joshua Peck:
Samuel Hickox: Jr
Josep Leuis
Abram Andrus:
John Andrus:
Tho Warner
John Hopkins
Edman Scott
John Welton sr
John Welton jr
Richard Welton
John Barns
Tho Welton
Tho Richards
Tho: Brounson
Isack Brounson Ju.

at a meting of the propry of Waterbury March 5,
1711.

6

it was greed on by by vote to burn aboutt the fens
on the west sid the River on thursday next and on the
est sid on friday next if thos not days fit the next
sesonabell days the Drum being. beat over nite

at the sam meting Zacery balding jur of milford was
admitted a propritor in habitant up on a bachelders
acomydation acording to the propriters act

att the same meting it was agred upon by vote that
al land that shal be granted from this time that shall
but on the common fens shall give liberty or liberty is
left to mak or mend the fens

att the same meting the propriters by vott gave to to
wiliam hickox and John Richards a pes of land on the
west sid of the River buting north one John Richards
land west on the comon fens south on wiliam hickox
land est on the River it not to pragedish hi wais and
former grants one this condistion they are to mak and
mantain forever fifty rods of fens in the comon line
at the north end of the fens now laid out

at the same meting thear was given to Richard
welton 6 or seaven acurs of land buting west and south
on hy waise noth one eprame warners orchard and a
strait line est to a pasig coms from a bogey madow and
est on said pasig

at the sam meting ther was granted to Isrell Richason
four acurs of land buting est and south on Richard
welton west and north on a hiway on condistions he
Relinqush four acurs of land formely granted to him
one the est sid his fathers mountan lot

att the same meting theare was granted to Isrell
Richason seaven acurs of land one the plane betwien
Isaac or barns madow and smith Judds madow on buks
hil on condistion he Relinkquish seven acurs of land
on pater Roon hill

att a meting of the propriters in waterbury ye march 5 1711 thear was chosen as a comity to go and view that land at brumsons madow in contry varsy betwien John brumson desesd and John hopkins and Richard porter: Isaac brumson snr abraham andrus snr dockter porter tho judd smith and bri[n]g Returns to the propriators in order to a setellment.

att the same meting ther was chosen John Richard william hickox and tho Judd smith a commity to vew som land west of John Richards eaight acr lot to fens for and lay out the fens they deem du and fifty rods mor to said Richards and hecox at the north end of the comon fens and vew what is after that is laid out what remains to do and bring Returns to the propriters in order to do it this year

att the same meting ebenezur Richason and benjimen Richards war admitted propriter in habytans and to have accomydation of land acording to the propriters act for bachildors

att the sam meting thear was granted to samll hickox and Joseph luis a pes of land west from scots medows at Judds medows one the hill west from Judd and Scovils lots for convenyans of fensing to met at a rok so south to the south sid scovils lot too or 3 acurs apees

at a meting of the propryters in waterbury September 18 1711 it was agrd upon by vote to clere the madows on 26 of september at night

at a meting of the propryters in Waterbury decembr 12th 1711 it was agred by a mager vote that the indien deeds be recorded in the book of Records at the propriters charg at the sam meting m^r John Soth maid dc thomas Judd was choson a comity to vew som writing of the grand comity and such as of valew to be Recorded the remainder to be obliterated

at the same meting Thomas Clark and ebennczur broumson ware admited propriter in habitans one a bacheldtors acomidation

at the same meting ther was granted to Thomas hickox al the land not alrady given him with in his fenc aganst the town land up stels brook

at the same meting the propritors gave william hickox a pes of land north of hickox broke one the west sid the river to but on his one land not to pregadish hi wais

at the same meting the propriters gave to danll warner a pes of land south of his land his hous stands on at Judds madows to but on samwell hickox land south not to pragadish hiwais

att a meting of the propriters in waterbury march 10 1712 the proprieters by vot agre to burn abought the fens on the west sid on tusday next on wensday on the est sid if sutabell days if not the next sutibel day the drum being beat over nite

at a meting of the propriters in Waterbury march 10 1712

Thomas barns jun steven hopkins and samll warner ware admitted a propryter inhabitant on a bacheldors acommydation acording to the propriters actt

at the same meting leften timothy stadly Isaac brunson jur Thomas Judd wer chosen a comity to lay out a cuntry rod to wards woodbury so far as our Bounds go

at the sam meting the propryters gave samll hickox
aight acurs of land at Judds madow south east of
Zacry balding lan on a hill estwardly from said medow
he Re link quich ing 5 acurs bogy medow and too of
upland at shesnut hill medow

at a meting of the propryters in waterbury sept
16, 1712, it was agreed upon by vot to cler the madows
for catell horses and shep by the next Saterday com
seven nit in the morning

at a meting of the propriators in waturs bry march
30ᵈ 1713: it is agred to burn for the: securing the fens
on the est sid the common feld next thursday to begin
at the northward so to go on one the west sid the next
day if the seson sut if not then the next sesun warning
to be given in the morning by beat of drum

at a meting of the propriaters in waturbury septembr 24 1713
[it] is agreed that the feld shall be commun for
cattel the 2ᵈ of october next

at a propritors meting held in waterburi desmbr
13 1713 obadiah scott was admited a propriator inhabitant on a bageldors acomidation right on that
accommidation that was baldens

at a propriators mting in waterbury in march 14ᵗʰ
1714 it was orderd to burn about the fence of the
common feeld one the east side on the 16ᵗʰ day of
this month and west sid on the 17ᵗʰ day on the north
end of the fence of the fore noon and the south sid
afternoon

Durham dember th8 1713   to The modarators of
Waterbury

I do for my propriyty and my fathers being propriator in sd township demand my Right in sd Township by division according to propriety and do by this
according To Right deny and Bar any grants of lands
In sd township to any so fare as the law justefy me in
any other way but according to propriaty and as for
what has ben given away since we came came away
and not have been warned To sd propriators meeting i
demand our right according to our propriaty and I
desir this may be recorded

Joseph gailord

At a propriators meting in Waterbury, Janiwary
18 1714/15

The propriators agreed by vote that the southe
ende of the bounds from the south west corner and
so to the east est of the bounds shall be measured

at the same meting there was chosen by vote for
to measure the sd bounds Mr. Southmaid left Timothy
Standly dec thomas Judd Dotor porter and william
hickox

At the same meting the propriators agred by vote
that theoese persons that have pitches or grants of
land shall have liberty from this present time to the
18 tenth of July to get Their land layd out and Recorded acording to law for neglect here of they are
to forfit all sd pitches or grants

At the same meting there [was] chosen by vote as a
comity decon Thomas Judd left timothy standly doct
porter to agree with Wallingford for the settlement of
the bounds

At the same meting It was agreed by vote that the

propriators shall defray the Charges that shall com
from laying out the sd bounds and if they cant agree
with walingford to go to cort about the bounds till it
hath a finall isshew

At the same meting there was granted to Thomas
Richason one acre and a half wher his hous now stands
the nor west side of his hous

At the same meting there was chosen for mesurers
Doctr Warner and John scovill

At the same meting there was chosen for to vew the
piches and compare them with the records to se whether
they agree with the records Is left standly decn Judd
doctr warner John Scovill John Judd

and the metting is dismist till the 2nd tuesday In
march

a propriators meting in Waterbury March the 14
1715 it was agreed by voat to burn about the fence of
the comon feild the first conveniant opertunity and
notis is to be given thereof by the beating the drum
in the morning

at the same metting it was acted by vote that within
five days from this present 14enth day of March the
feeld is to be closed of all catell hogs and sheep and
the fences to be done up

March the 8 1715

a propriators meting held in Waterbury and there
was inacted by voat that for burning about the fence
decon Judd causing the drum to bete over night it is
to be & the next day following to burne aboute the
weste side fence & after the weste sid fence is burnt
about it is furder left to the decon judd to give notese

for burning aboute the east side fence by the same warning that is above riten for the west sid fence

At the same meting it was inacted by the proprietors by vote that ye fence vewars sholld be sent out the ninth of March 1715 . . . to clear the comon field . . . creatures that are pound feasante the hawards are to be sent oute on ther ofice work and so to pound acording to the derection of the law   and so the meeting is agarned tell th 2 tuseday of aprill next

The third line of the seconte acte is so enterlined that it cante be very well red it is to be understood that on the 15tenth day of this present month above mentioned that by vote of the proprators that the comon feelds shold be don up that is to say all the fence and the hawerds are to be sent oute upon there ofice work

At meting of the propriators april 12 = 1705 (1715) And the propriators acted by voat to gett the county measurer to mesure the southerd end of the bounds from the southwest corner of the bounds and so to mesure east Tel he hath got the biredeth acording to Chayter (charter)

A proprietors meeting held in Waterbury april 12. 1715 And it was inacted by voat that the land formerly granted to the bachelldors shall be ther one exsept ing thos that have not fulfild the condistions nor like to fulfill them. 2nd we agre that all the grants of land formerly given by the town and propritors shall stand good

3 = we agree that avery originall propritor shall have too bachell ders acomodations to each lott if he has not had it formerly by him self al grants of land

given out of the undevided land to be computted to mak this bacheldurs acomidation and what is wanting to be mad up out of the undevided land

And after that mak a devistion of one hundred acurs apeis to each origonall propriter and bacheldors acomdation to each of them alike and the remander of the undevided land to be devided to the originall propriters acording to meadow alot mentt

it is to be understood that thos originall propriters have sons that have had grants to them formerly given them of bachelders acomidations they shall count it one ther fathers writ and counted to them as one or too now granted: and then the 40 pound proprity formerly granted to be void and of non efect: thomas clark bacheldors accomidation to be one of lft timothy standlys his too Rits

John welton jur gorg scot and david scot are admited bachillders to the 100 acur devistion to each of them

it was further agred upon by vote that this act shall be counted as adevistion

dc danill porter protests aganst said actt

at the same meting doter warner and richard wellton was chosen to lay out the highways at bux hill acording to their best scill

At the same meting leften John Standly desiered by the propriators by act of voat To recorde the indians deed of this Town

and the meeting is agarned till the seckond toused day in november next

at the same meting abraham andrus and srgnt stephen upson was chosen a comitty to lay out the country road from the mill River begining at the paith that goeth over the river a letel westward of the mill and so as fare as the ende of the bounds that is to say tell they com to new haven bounds

To the propriator inhabitance of Waterbury asembled April 12—1715

brethren and nabours I the subscriber haveing to grate dissatisfaction observed the way of your giveing or granting away of land To bring in inhabitance according to an act mad for that porpos upon record desembr 20–1697 which hath a derect tendensy to vialate and destroy and conterary to right ecquity and justis or any well digested reson to invaid the property of the first purchasers i supose it to be a truth not to be gainsayed that Those that were the first purchesurs ofthe land within the township did thereby aquire aright according to the propotion of what payments they made by order of the comity for the setling of the place and the articles they fullfilled and to be subdevided as is at large comprised in the pattin to the then present propriator inhabitanc and their heirs I have no where seen that the antient propriators did impower the mager part by voat to give the land at their plesure the received prinsiple I perceave if I mistake not is that the majer parte of the propriators in comon may by voat when aposed by the miener give away from the miener when and as they pleas that which is consequent upon it is that the major may combien and give it all to and amongst them selves so that the miener shall have nither land nor comonig I supose it to be treu that ther hath been grate opisitions by som of the antient propriators agnst granting land according to sd act for my own part to my best remembrance I have never been warned to any propriators meeting [   ] or at the making sd act in 1697 be

sure I was not there [   ] to my knowlidg others
have not been warned as they have told me [   ] the
whole I take this opertunity to declare and protest
[   ] propriators proseeding any father in giveing
[or] granting any more in [   ] any purticolure
person or persons and allso i do protest against [   ]
grants that have been made according to sd act to
make [   ] inhabitance i have hereunto sett my
hand as one of [the paten]tese and one of the first
propriators and were posesed [of one hund]red pound
right of my own and by a distribution of john [newels]
estate all his right in the outlands fell to me pray let
there be no strife between us we obtain and fullfild
articles how you came to have a right to dispose of it
i know not

    witnes Jerimiah peck   John Standley
    Thomas Clark

    at a proprietors meting in waterbury September
the 30–1715 it was agreed by the proprietors by voate
that the comon feilds shold be clerd by the forth day
of october next at night
    at the same meting the propriators by vote im-
powered dec thomas judd and Insin john hopkins in
case that if Wallingford will not agree with the comitty
that was chosen in jenanury 18–17$\frac{14}{15}$ for them to
manige it at the next jenerall cort according to their
best scill

A propriators meeting In waterbury november the
9–1715 And it was acted by voat that all the originell
propriters should tak up aight acres of their bachelders
lots in the sequestered land that is to say of those lots
that was granted to the originall proprietors in april

12 = 1715—not to pregedis highways and former grants

at the same meeting There was granted by voate that the olde proprietors have liberty to take the sd bacheldors acomidation by there one land and in case they dont take it up by their one land it is to be layd out with the hundred acre devition

at the same meeting there was granted a hundred and fifty pound propriety In the undevided land for to be cept for the menestry that is for the town for to dispose on for the use of the ministry

at the same meeting it was agreed upon by voat that the alotment of one hundred acers apeace to the origanal propriators and the bacheldors right belonging to them and to the bacheldors acomidation agreed on april the 12–1715 shall begin on the south west corner of our bounds next to Woodbury bounds and the length of the teer of lots to be a mille In length east and west and to run north on sd woodbury Line unteel they hauf half the number of acers and then on the east of sd teer a highway twenty rods wide and then another teer of lots south to derby bounds which teer shall be a mile in length as the first teer was and the high ways east and west throug the teer four rods wide and the placeing them we leave to the decretion of the layers out

and the meeting is dismist till the 2nd teusday in desember (?) next

To the propriators of the Township of Waterbury being ascembled in a propriators meeting at sd town in novembr 8th day 1715

gentn I take leave to tell you my minde respecting the undout[ed] Right that the originall propriators

to sd town of Waterbury had unto the sd township
which doth still belong to sd origenal propriators or
their heirs that legally represent them of whome I am
one and forasmuch as a part of the proprietors of sd
town do pretend to a power of granting of land to the
damig of severall of the propriators therefore I the
subscriber hereof do now publickly as a legall propriator
of the lands of sd town in this open meeting declare
and protest against sd Illegall proseedings and by this
proceeding I do fully declare and protest against all
granting or disposing the lands In sd town any other
way but by ane equall devition according To every
propriators right as in the origanall grant made and
confirmed by pattent from the generall assembly   In
testimony whereof I have here unto sett my hand the
day and year above writen

Stephen hickox

signed in presence of
Jams wadsworth
Jeremiah Lemin

at a propriators meeting in Waterbury Desembr the
13–1715 and it was acted by voat that all the names of
the origanall propritors shall be entered in the book
of records

at the same meeting there was chosen as a comity
for finde ho ar the proper originall propriators and to
enter in the book of records as is above exspreste is dc
john standly Abraham andrus insin john hopkins and
john judd

at a meeting of the proprietors in Waterbury december the 13–1715
and so contineued by agrnment tell the 16tnh day of

the month above Sd and it was acted by voate for the laying out of the devetions of lands leften timothy standly to lay out the easte side of the river and to that quarter of the bounds from farmingtown road southward and so on the east side the river from farmingtown road northward dotr ephreham warner and for the [west] sid of the river northward from woodbury road Decn thomas Judd and on the west side the river southward John Scovill

at the same meeting there was granted a rate of eight pounds as mony to defray the charge that hath been exspended and the overplus To be laid out on what charge shall be afterward.

at the same meeting there was granted by voat to Thomas wellton libertie to relinquish the teen acres that was his fathers lying by the west side the long swamp and to take it up on the west side of Turkie brok on a brok that cometh from the east side of hickox mountain and runs into turcky brok.

and the meeting is ajurned tell the 2cond tuesday of april in the year 1716

a meeting of the propriators in waterbury april 10–1716

It was agreed upon by voat that those propriators that are gon from us that were admited in the year 1697 and sence in the year one thousand seven hundred two three shall have their land that they have improved according to sd grant—and no more and those that were admited sence february 170⅔ and have lived in the town in a constant way five years after and built a hous according To sd act may have the holl of his bachelldors lot and those of both that have not fullfilled according to sd acts nor in a way to fullfill we

do now tak the forfiture of them exsepting those admited in desmber–13–1715

at the same meeting it was actid by voat that there
shold be a small Book prepared for the yong bacheldors
at the begining of it the conditions that they are to
fullfill and then under that their lots to be recorded
and so to stand tell they have fullfilld

at the same meeting left timothy standly and william
hickox were chosen as a comity to lay out the sequestered land and to vew the high way that leads to
farmingtown against david scott's lot at the mad
river and pas their their judgments concerning the
[   ] in of the hig way and mak return to the town

at the same meeting ther was chosen as a comity
dc thomas judd srg [stephen] upson John scovill for
to lay out the fence to such lands within the [common]
feeld that have not had fence laid to it allredi and the
remainders of the [fence to] be done by the propriators
for this year

at a meeting of the propriators in Waterbury, April
10–1716

And it was acted by voat that william judd taillor
shold have a piece of land between hancox medow and
hickox holes aplain peace of land the whole of sd plain
if he fence for sd land according to the lands in the
comon feeld—and the meeting is agrnd to the 2cond
teusda of desembr—

at a meeting of the propriators in waterbury may
8 1716 it was agreed upon by a full voat in adtion to
voat jenewary 18–17$\frac{5}{16}$ and a voat of the propriators
septembr 30–1715 they now firder impower thomas
judd Lftent john hopkins to act In our behalf at the

next generall [Court] in the [   ] instant may for
agreement of the bounds at the south east corner wher
we sopose walingford intrudes on us and do there in as
they think fit and what they do there in we except
as don by us

a propriators meting in waterbury in desembr the
11 1716 and nevery act pased only the meeting was
againned to the grate meeting day of the month afore
sd to begin at son an oure high in the after noone

a proprietors meeting in Waterbury desmbr the 20
1716
and it was acted by voat that the yong propriators
land shal be recorded in the 2cond book of records with
the provisiall or conditions that the propriators laid
on the sd bachelldor elotments
At the same meeting the propriators agreed by
voat to make chois of as a comity Cptn Thomas Judd
Leften John hopkins and Srgnt John Brounson to
agree with the propriators of Wallingford for a finall
issue of [the matter] between Waterbury and Wallingford conserning our b[ounds and we] impower the
above sd comity To Compremise the m[atter and to]
agree with them and setle the matter by seting[   ]
bound marks according to law and what they do [
we will   ] account as done by our selves And the
meeting [was adjourned to] the first mun day of
March [   ]
dotr daniell portr did protest against the yong propriators having their lands Recorded in the book of
records—and Edman Scott at the same Time protested against the sd act.

at a meting of the propryitors in waterbury march
4 1717

it was agreed on by vote to leve the time of burning
about the fens about the comon feeld to John richards
John Scovell with the moderator and to give notis
by beting the drum ovr nite and if the day folowing be
good then to beat in the morning if not not fit to beat
the drum and to burn on the west sid north in the fore
none and south afer none the next day if good wather
north in [the] foore none and south in the aftr none
on est sid

the above ritten act shll stand in force yeare 1718
this act shall stand till 1719

the sam meting it was agrd by vote that the remainder of the fens that the land will not do that is
or shall be modalized by the comity shall be don by the
propriters to inclos the comon field

at the same meting the propriatores agre by vote:
that they will: send a sitation to the propriators of
walingford and goo: on with our petetion to the next
generall cort to be holden at haford in may next insew-
ing in ordor to seteling the bounds betwen wallingford
and waterbury Pro Propriators

This meeting is agurnd to 12th day of instant
March

At a meating of the propriators on december ye
14 1720 where as Left John hopkins and John Scovill
formerly chosen moderators and the records not being
full and play[n] to explain what was intended we the
propriators of Waterbury do caus and declair by vote
that the fore sd Cap John Hopkins and John Scovll Jr
shall have power to act joyntly or severly as modrators
to lead in the affares of propriatary concerns in com-

7

mon lands or in things of that nature pased in the meeting

the moderators ajurnd the meeting to the first tusday of febewary next insuing the date hereof

and the propriators of Waterbury met according to ajurnmente which was the seaventh day of febewary 1721 at the same meeting there was chosen for a comity cap judd left hopkins and left timothy stanly to sarch · the records and finde out what bachelurs have fulfild articles and whoo have not fulfild articles and make returns to the propriators

it was agreed by vote that they would ajurn the meeting till tomorrow morning till eaight oclock in the morning

and the propriators of Waterbury met acording to ajurnmente which was on the 8th day of Febewary 1721

at the same meating the propriators agree by vote that for the futur the town mesurer shall not lay out any land to any person but whats theire due and that they shall receive order frome the town clark for what theay lay out from time to time

at the same meating there was chosen by vote for town mesurs with ser John Scovell and ensighn william hikcox to asist them in laying out land for the propriators william judd to lay out land with Ser John Scovell and thomas clark to lay out land with ensighn william hikcox

at a meating of ye propriators in waterbury february ye 8: 1721 it is agreed by vote that each oregenall propriator that is a 100 pound propriaty shall have too bachulers acomedations if they have not had them

themselves nor there sons had them out of the undevided land and so proportionable for greater or leser
propriaty on conditions they build and live heare acording to the articles 1697 and 170$\frac{2}{3}$ or els to forfit
there rites and then upon the bachuldors now made
propriators when fulfild articles and those formerly
admited that have fulfild articles with the origanall
propriators to devide all the undivided land acording
to propriaty from time to time as they shall agree
both to oreginall and bachelders propriaty and noe
other ways Thomas Clark is acounted as upon lft
timothy standly bacheldors rite
  the propriators ajurnd the meating to the laste
tusday in febewary next insuing the date hereof

  we being apointed a comety to macke sarch to
finde out who ware admited upon bachulders acomedations and who have fulfilled the codetions to maike
the land theire own and who hav not fulfild the articles
february 8 1721

those that have fulfiled agreements

William hikcox	thomas Richards	
Joseph gaylard	gorg Scott	these on a 40
John gaylard	david Scott	pound pro-
John warner sen	John Welton	priaty when
Thomas Richason	Ebenezer Richason	we devided
John Brunson sen	benjamin Richards	
Isarael Richason	thomas barns	
Stephen Wellton	Stephen hopkins	
Joseph hikcox	obadiah Scott	
Roberd Scott	ebenezer brunson	
John Richasen	thomas clark	
Thomas hikcox	John barns	

Richard welton
Benjamin warner
Isaac Brunson
Eprim warner
Samuell Standly
Benjamin Barns jur
Thomas Welton

thomas brunson
Joseph lewis
obadiah richards
abraham andrus jur
Joseph Brunson
Stephen ubson jur
Nathaniel Richason

those admited that have
not fulfild but in a likely
　way
John Scovell
Jonathan Scott jur
John Standly jur
William Judd
daniel porter jur
John Judd
timo thy Standly ser
timothy hopkins
gorg Scott jur
John hikcox
Samuel Scott
thomas ubson
thomas andrus
benjamin warner jur
Samuell porter
Ebenezr hikcox
John Richards j ır
gorg welton
thease in the above collum
have not as yet fulfild but
are in ye way to fulfill the
articles on which they
ware ad mitted

those that have not fulfiled
　as we judg
William gaylord
John warner tailer
Stephen hikcox
moses brunson
daniel porter son
of richard

Timothy standly ⎫
John hopkins　⎬ comety
Thomas Judd　 ⎭

at a meating of the pro-
priators of Waterbury febewary 8 1721 thay agred by
vote to axsepte ye return
of the comety and order it
to be entered upon record

At a meating of the propriators of Waterbury in Waterbury October 9 1721 Lft John hopkins and ensighn william hikcox presente debuties for Waterbury ware made choise of to answer in theire behalf to the petition of Left John mash (marsh) John beuell and John Bard of Litchfield broughte againste the town of Waterbury as propriators and cited to answare it at the generall court holden in new haven on the second thirsday in October instante

Waterbury February 27 The Proprietors Meet According To Adjournment As It Was Adjurned February 28th 1720/1   The Meeting was Adjourned to to-morrow at eight Clock to Meet at Serg^t Scovills. February 28th the proprietors in Waterbury Meet According to Adjournment   It was Agreed upon by vote that whereas an Act In February 8th 1721 was grevious to Some of our proprietors we now Further Agree that Every originall proprietor or propriety shall have two Bachelor Lots upon an hundred pounds propriety and proportionally upon Greater and lesser proprietyes with what was granted last February notwithstanding what their sons have had which bacheldor Lott Is Looked upon now to be now 68 Acres   And a forty pound propriety And the Obligation upon those granted In February 8th 1721 and now granted to be taken off and be free from Any Incumberance of building and cohabiting.

And then Grant to the Bacheldors that were admited upon a forty pound propriety that they Shall have as a Division of fifty-five Acres to every bacheldor that has fulfilled articles or In Away to fullfill articles, as they are returned by a Committy appointed In February and Recorded In the old proprietors Book.

and for the future our Devisions shall be made upon Originall proprietors with the addition made to their propriety and upon bacheldor proprietors According to their propriety and It is the true Intent and meaning of the proprietors In this act and shall be so taken and Explained that Every original propriety of one hundred pounds shall have two bacheldor proprietyes and no more and so proportionably for Greater or Leser proprieties and that all devisions of All our Lands after this shall be made upon the present Original proprietors and bacheldor proprietors that are all ready made.

this A bove was voted by the proprietors

At the same meeting Cap. Thomas Judd and Serg[t] John Scovill were chosen A Committy with the Clerk to Make a List of the Originall and bacheldor proprietors to make a division of our Land upon.

The meeting was Adjurned to the 2[d] Tuseday In March 1722 to Meet at the meeting-house at Eight A Clock In the Morning.

March 13, 1722. the Proprietors Mett According to Adjurnment March 13, 1722. the proprietors by vote A Gree that Gershom Fulford shall have a Lott with us to Direct him when to take up the Land that Is Given him by Subscription and to take It up In one peice and In a handsome form.

The meeting Adjourned to the 14 day Instant at 8[t] clock morning to meet At the Meeting house.

The Propriators Mett March 14 1722 According to Adjournment.

At a meeting of the proprietors for Waterbury

March 14 1722. It was by vote Agreed that the Land granted as A Division to certain Originall and Bacheldor proprietors Att a meeting of the proprietors In Waterbury Feb. 28 1721² they shall have Liberty to take It up by their own Land and In one place more and In a handsome Form.

At the Same Meeting Timothy Hopkins was Chosen Measurer.

At the Same meeting It was Enquired wheither there Is any Land to be Laid out to the Original proprietors more yn 68 acres upon A bacheldors Right upon upon A fifty pound propriety In this division. It was voated that there Is but 68 acres.

At the Same Meeting It was by vote Agreed that Every man that has Land Laid out according to the Act of the proprietors shall have but one note to the measurers Signed by the Recorder for the Land that he has to lay out. And Every Measurer shall Indors upon the note what Land Is Laid out upon that note and yr shall be Arecord made of Every note that goes out of the Office.

At the Same Meeting It was Agreed by vote that one measurer shall be Impowered to Lay out Land not with Standing Any Act that has [been passed] to the Contrary. and they shall be Divided A measurer to Each [quarter] that is to say Sergᵗ Scovill on the west Side of the River and [south of] Woodbury Road William Judd on the west side of the River [north] of Woodbury Road. Ensign Hikcox on the East side of the Riv[er north] of the Road that goes to Farmington and Timothy Hopkins [on the] East Side of the River and South of Farmington Road that go[es by] Beaver pond. and the Measurers In yr Returns shall note [the] bounderies the Length and breadth of the Land the number of Acres and upon what Account they **Lay** It out.

At the Same Meeting It was by vote Agreed that when A measurer has land to lay out In his own quarter for him self he shall Call one of the other measurers to Lay out his own Land.

At the Same Meeting Capt. Thomas Judd and Joseph Lewis were Appointed A committy to Attend and Inspect the Committy appointed by the Generall Court upon Litchfields petition and represent the proprietors and Inform them Concerning our line at the South End when the Committy shall Come upon that Business

At the Same meeting it was agreed that the measurers In laying out of land shall consider what highways are needful and leave Land for highways accordingly

The propriators Meeting Is adjourned to the Last tuseday In October next.

Att Ameeting of the Proprietors of Waterbury in Waterbury May 7 1722. there was Appointed as a Committy Capt Thomas Judd Lif^t John Hopkins, John Richards, Serg^t John Scovill, William Judd to Agree and Settle boundaries between Waterbury and Litchfield and so by our Act Impower the sd Committy to Make A final Issue of that Matter with the Committy that shall be Appointed from Litchfield.

Att the Same Meeting Capt Thomas Judd with the Deputies of Waterbury were Appointed a Committe to Carry the Case between Litchfield and Waterbury to the Generale Court and represent us there.

Waterbury October 30th 1722, the proprietors meet According to Adjurnment In March 14th 1722: The

Day spent without doing Anything but adjurning the Meeting to 31st Instant at Eight OClock in the morning.

A A meeting of the propriators of Waterbury Meet by Adjurnment October 31, 1722. It was by vote Agreed that those papers that Deacon John [Standly] shall present Setting forth the Acts of the Grand Committe [relating] to the setling of the town shall be Recorded that Is to [say those] of them that dont appear to be All ready Recorded and [we here] by Impower the Clerk to record them. And those that are not [deemed] Needfull shall be returned to Deacon Standly Againe.

this vote Entered and Examined by me

John Southmayd Clerk

At the Same Meeting It was Agreed by vote that there shall at the next proprietors meeting, one Hundred and fifty acres of the undivided land, which is not sequistered, be sould to the highest bidder and the money lodged In Safe hands and to be disposed of for the defraying of the proprietors publick Charges that has All ready been and not yet paid and what shall hereafter Arise so far as It shall Go that Is to say the Charges since the year 1718 and forward.

this vote Entered and Examined by me

John Southmayd Clerk.

Att the Same Meeting It was Agreed by vote that we will proceed to A devision of the sequestred Land In the north west quarter of the bounds upon the proprietors, and propriety as they were made and Setled In Feb. 8th 1721 and In Feb. 28th 1721².

A true Record of the vote.

Attest. Jnº Southmayd Clerk.

Att the Same meeting It was Agreed that we will prepare for A Lott as soon as may be, and do hereby

Impower Serg^t John Scovill with the town Clerk A Committe to Make a List of the proprietors Seting forth Each mans propriety as Stated by the Above mentioned Acts and to be laid before the proprietors at their next meeting for to be Considered and approved by them.

    A true Record of the vote

                Attest. Jn° Southmayd Clerk.

    The Meeting was adjurned to the Last Tuesday In November next.

                    G. S. K.[1]

  [1] God Save the King (?)

Proprietors' Records from "First
Book of Town Meetings"
November 27, 1722—Last Monday of
March, 1761

Proprietors' Records

Att A meeting of the proprietors In Waterbury November 27, 1722.

It was A Greed by vote that the Severall Acts of the proprietors from this time Forward Shall All wayes be entered In the Town Book. or the Book that Is made use of to Record In Att town Meetings In Waterbury.

A true Record of the Vote.

A:test John Southmayd Clerk.

Att the Same Meeting It was Agreed by A vote, that In the Devision of the Sequestred Land att the North West Corner of the bounds. It Shall be divided upon the Originall proprietors as they are Entred In the Second book of Records and the addition made to them and upon the proprietors as they are Entred upon this Sheet with the addition of Six forty pound proprieties which must ly for the proprietors use And do here by Impower the Committe when they Lay out the A bove S^d Six Lotts to take possession of them for the proprietors.

A true Record of the vote.

Attest John Southmayd, Clerk.

Att the Same meeting It was Agreed by vote that In the Deviding of the Sequestred Land At the North west Corner there Shall be three tears of Lotts. Viz. A high way Next Woodbury of two Rods wide, and then half A mile wide of land to be Laid out In Lotts And then A high way of Eight Rods to run North and

South and then Another tear of half Amile wide And then Another high way of Eight Rods. and then Another tear of Lotts half Amile wide and then A high way on the East Side of Eight Rods. and when we begin to Lay out the Lots. the first Lott Shall be-Gin at the South End of the West tear and So Successively till that tear Is Laid out and then Come down with the Lotts In the Second tear And then to Go up with the Lotts In the third tear and So to finish the Lotts at the north End of the East tear and the Committe In Laying out the Lotts to Leave A four or Six Rod High way Every half mile or there A bout through the tears no Lott to be Divided.

A true Record of the vote

Attest. John Southmayd Clerk.

Att the Same meeting It was by vote Agreed that the 150 Acres Agreed up on the Last meeting to be Sould at this Meeting Shall be offered upon Sale tomorrow and 50 Acres at A time till the 150 be Sould If Chapmen Appear.

And do Impower Capt Thomas Judd Capt Worner Richard Welton George Scott Se^r Thomas Clerk A Committe to make Sale of the A bove S^d Land and order A note from the Clerk to the measurers to Lay out the Land to him that buys In order to Its being Laid out to them that buy, In order to their Geting It recorded and Setled upon them and their Heirs.

A true Record Attest. John Southmayd Clerk.

The meeting adJurned till to morrow.

November. 28 1722. Land Sould at A van due fifty Acres at A time the first fifty Acres Sould to Doc. Daniell Porter which was the highest bidder at 5^sh and 6^d p Acre which Comes to—   13 . 15 = 00.

The Second fifty Acres Sould to Doc Daniell Porter who was the highest bidder at Six Shillings Six pence p Acre.   16 = 05—00

The third fifty Acres Sould at Avandue to Doc Daniell Porter who was the highest bidder Sould at 6^{sh}. 6^d. p Acre.   16 = 05—00

                              Total   46 = 05—00

Sould by order of the proprietors as appears by the Above Entred Act of Novem. 27. 1722. by us

Thomas Judd

Ephraim Worner

Richard Welton   ⎬   Committe

George Scott

Thomas Clark

Att A meeting of the proprietors Waterbury Novem^{er} 28 1722. Met by Adjurnment the proprietors Agree In order to the Drawing of the Lott orderly that Cap Judd and Capt Worner and Lif. Hopkins Shall have the Man age-Ment of the Lott when It Is Drawn to Call to the Lott See what Lott is drawn And Give order for It to be Entered by the Clerk

A true Record of the vote.

Attest. John Southmayd Clerk.

Att the Same Meeting It was by vote Agreed that there Shall be an Entry made of the Lott. that Is drawn for and they Shall be Entred as the Lott fell. 1. 2. 3 and So forth and Each ones propriety aded to his Name to be Entred In the town book where we Enter our proprietors Acts.

A true Record Attest. John Southmayd Clerk.

Att the Same Meeting It was by vote Agreed that the Committe that Shall be Chosen to Lay out the Devision Now Agreed upon Shall not Go upon the

Work till the first of Aprill Next to Lay out the Lots
and to lye by the work and to have three Shillings
and Six pence per day mony
A true Record Attest. John Southmayd Clerk.

Att the Same Meeting was Chosen for A Committe
to Lay out the Lott Lift Hikcox Richard Welton
John Judd George Welton Cap Thomas Judd William
Judd.
A true Record Attest. John Southmayd Clerk.

Att the Same Meeting was Chosen for A proprietors
Treasurer John Southmayd to Receive the Mony of
the Committe that they Sould the Land for: which
treasurer Shall Give A Recept of the Mony Received
and not pay out Any Money but upon Sight of A Bill.
Signed by A Committe that Shall be Chosen and Atrue
Account kept of the disbursements to be Laid before
the proprietors.
A true Record Attest. John Southmayd Clerk.

Att the Same Meeting It was by vote Agreed that
Moses Brounson of Stratford Shall be Accepted upon
that Bacheldors Lott that was formerly Granted him
he SubScribing to the Articles In 1697 & 1702³
A true Record Attest. John Southmayd Clerk.

Att the Same Meeting I Moses Brounson of Stratford
In the County of Fairfeild do by these oblidge my Self
to perform Articles According to the Acts of the proprietors In 1697 & 1702³ or Else to for fit what Is
Now Granted me   In witness where of I have here
unto Set my hand In presence of Witnesses

John Southmayd   Moses Brounson
Ephraim Worner
A true Record Attest. John Southmayd Clerk.

Att the Same Meeting It was by vote Agreed that
the Grant of 30 Acres to the old Saw mill proprietors

Shall Stand Good only they Shall be oblidged to take It In the undivided Land. In one peice or Every one to take his part of the 30 Acres by his own Land. A true Record Attess. Jn°. Southmayd Clerk.

Att the Same Meeting It was by vote Agreed that John Worner Son of Ephraim and William Scott both of Waterbury Shall be accepted on the Bacheldors Right that was formerly Granted to Daniel Porter Son of Richard Porter they Severally Subscribing to perform Articles According to the Act In 1697 & 1702[3]

A true Record Attess. John Southmayd Clerk.

Att the Same meeting was Chosen for A Committe to Sign Bills to Draw money out of the treasury Lift John Hopkins Thomas Hikcox and John Richards or Any two of them.

A true Record Attest John Southmayd Clerk

The Meeting AdJurned to the Last Tuseday of November Next.

A List of the Lott as It was Drawn for A Devision of the Sequestred Land Att the North west Quarter of the bounds. Nov. 28 1722.

the Lott		the propriety
1	Daniell Porter. Son. Daniell.	40
2	William Hikcox	40
3	Joseph Hikcox	108
4	John Hikcox	40
5	Benjamin Richards	40
6	Samuell Hikcox Se^r.	180
7	Lif. John Hopkins	180
8	Joseph Gailard Ju^r.	40
9	John Brounson. of. Isaac	40
10	John Judd Ju^r.	40
11	Johnathan Scott Ju^r.	40

8

the Lott		the propriety
12	Robert Scott	40
13	Edmun Scott Ju^r.	126
14	Thomas Worner	180
15	Abraham Andruss Copper	180
16	Isaac Brounson. Se^r.	180
17	David Scott.	40
18	Obadiah Scott	40
19	Stephen Upson Se^r.	90
20	Joseph Hikcox Ju^r.	40
21	Benjamin Worner Se^r.	40
22	John Worner Se^r.	162
23	John Standly Se^r.	180
24	Thomas Judd Ju^r.	180
25	Edmun Scott Se^r.	180
26	Timothy Hopkins	40
27	Thomas Welton	40
28	Richard Porter.	90
29	Stephen Welton	40
30	George Scott Se^r.	40
31	Samuell Standly	40
32	John Scovill Ju^r.	40
33	Phillip Judd	144
34	John Carington.	108
35	the first proprietors Lott.	40
36	the Second proprietors Lott.	40
37	Stephen Hopkins.	40
38	Benjamin. Bernes. Se^r.	180
39	Daniell Worner	108
40	John Brounson Se^r.	144
41	Thomas Clark	40
42	John Bernes	40
43	Ebenezar Hikcox	40
44	C^t. Thomas. Judd. William.	180
45	School Lott	270

the Lott		the propriety
46	Nathaniell Richason	40
47	George Scott Ju^r.	40
48	Timothy Standly. Or.	180
49	Capt. Thomas Judd. Jones.	180
50	Ebenezar Richason	40
51	Abraham Andruss Ju^r.	40
52	Thomas Richason. Se^r.	90
53	Obadiah Richards Ju^r	40
54	Josep Lewis	40
55	Thomas Handcox	180
56	Mr Jeremiah Peck	270
57	John Welton Se^r.	144
58	William Judd	40
59	John Gailard	40
60	Ebenezar Brounson	40
61	John Richason	40
62	Joseph Gailard Se^r.	144
63	Daniell Porter Se^r.	171
64	the 5th pro Lott Moses Brounson	40
65	Stephen Upson Ju^r.	40
66	Samuell Porter	40
67	John Scovill Se^r.	144
68	John Richards Se^r.	144
69	Thomas Richards Se^r.	40
70	Thomas Bernes	40
71	John Judd Se^r.	180
72	Abraham Andrus Se^r.	144
73	Benjamin Worner Ju^r.	40
74	John Welton Ju^r.	40
75	Thomas Hikcox	40
76	the 4th pro Lott. to Jno Worner. W. Scott.	40
77	John Southmayd	270
78	Lift Timothy Standly: Bach^e	40

the Lott		the propriety
79	Richard Welton	40
80	Samuell Worner. of Thomas.	40
81	Joseph Brounson	$40
82	George Welton	40.
83	Thomas Newell.	$162.
84	Thomas Upson	40.
85	Isaac Brounson Ju^r.	40
86	150^{lb} prpriety	150
87	Israell Richason	40
88	Samuell Scott	40
89	Thomas Andruss	40
90	Thomas Richason Ju^r.	40
91	John Richards Ju^r.	40
92	Thomas Brounson	40
93	Jonathan Scott. Se^r.	90
94	John Newell.	180
95	Ephraim Worner	40
96	Benjamin Bernes Ju^r.	40
97	the 3^d prop Lott	40
98	Obadiah Richards Se^r.	144
99	John Worner Se^r Bach Lott	40
100	the 6th pro Lott.	40
101	John Stanly Ju^r.	40

We John Worner Son of Ephraim Worner and William Scott both of Waterbury being admited Bacheldor proprietors by An Act of the proprietors In November 28 1722. upon A forfited Right formerly Granted to Daniell Porter Son of Richard porter of Waterbury we do by these oblidge our Selves. to perform Articles according to the Act of the proprietors In 1697. and In 1702³ by Each of us living here the term and building According to the Dementions.   In witness where of we have here unto Set our hands. this 31 January Anno Domini. 1722³.

In presence of.   John worner
John Southmayd Clerk.   Willam Scott

Waterbury March 4ᵗʰ 1723.   We the Committe Capᵗ. Thomas Judd Capᵗ. Ephraim Worner George Scott Seʳ. Richard welton Thomas Clerk appointed to make Sale of the 150 Acres of Land ordered to be Sold to Defray the proprietors Charges and did Make Sale of It to Doctor Daniell Porter November 28. 1722. upon his Engaging the Money or Bond Within Fourteen dayes After the Sale which Condition the Doctor Refuseing or failing. and Also. unto us the Above Sᵈ Committe and before us all, the Sᵈ Porter did, on March 1. 1722³ resign all his Right In the Above Sᵈ Land to be disposed of by us for the use Above Sᵈ we do there fore take the Land Into our own hand to dispose of to the use Above Sᵈ and do Declare the Doctor has no Right In the Above Sᵈ Land upon that Sale but It is utterly voide and of None Effect. and Shall have no note from us or order for the Land as the Acts Direct in order to to his haveing title thereunto upon that Sale   In wit ness where of we have hereunto Set our hands

Thomas Judd
ephraim warner
His
Signed in presence of   George Scott   } Committe
John Southmayd Clerk.   mark
Richard Wellton
Thomas Clarke

Att A Meeting of the Proprietors of **Waterbury**

Novemb^r 26th 1723. then John Southmayd was
Chosen Proprietors Clerk And Sworn.

Att the Same Meeting the proprietors by their vote
did Appoint as A Committe Doc Porter Isaac Brounson
Joseph Lewis to Consider and Inspect Certain Difficulties Laid before the proprietors with Respect to
some Grants under difficulties and make A return to
the proprietors. that the Matter may be Settled by
the proprietors.

A true Record of the Vote.

Attes^d. John Southmayd Clerk.

Att the Same Meeting It was by vote Agreed. that
wewill go upon A devision of our undivided Land. In
two Devisions Among the present proprietors In the
Method Following that Is to Say the first Devision
half an Acre on the pound. and the Second Devision
half an Acre on the pound to be taken up by A Lott
and one Lott drawn Shall regulate the taking up both
the Devisions that Is to Say he that Draws the first
Lott. Shall take the first Lott In the first Devision
and the last Lott In the Second Devision and the
Last Lott Drawn Shall have the Last Lott In the
first Devision and the first Lott In the Second Devision
and Accordingly Every man Shall have his Lott and
In his turn Every man to Accomodate him self. Shall
have Liberty to Lay It in Severall peices by his own
Land hand Somely formed and where men dont Lay
It by y^r own Land they Shall Lay It In one peice and
In A handsome form.

A True Record of the vote.

Attes^d. John Southmayd Clerk.

Waterbury November 26. 1723.

Att the Same Meeting It was by vote Agreed that
where proprieties are broaken and Destributed Among

Heirs, they Shall have Liberty to take It up with their own proper Lott If they have A right and to take It up as they do their own Lott.—
A true Record of the vote.
Attes. John Southmayd Clerk.

Att the Meeting of the proprietors In Waterbury November 26 1723. we the Committe that Disposed of the 150 Acres to Doc Daniell Porter. and did on his failure take the Land In to our own hands Again do declare before the proprietors that we do resign our power of Committe and the 150 Acres again Into the hands of the proprietors to be disposed by them as they See Cause In Witness where of we Sett to our hands.

Thomas Judd
Signed before   Ephraim Worner
John Southmayd   George Scott. + His mark
Proprietors Clerk.   Richard Welton
Thomas Clark.
A true Record Attes. John Southmayd Clerk.
Att the Same Meeting the proprietors did by vote accept the resignment of the Committe—
A true Record Attest. John Southmayd Clerk.
Att the Same Meeting It was by vote Agreed that to pay what money the proprietors are at present Indebted and what Charges Shall Arise upon the Laying out the North west Corner of the bounds all ready drawn for there Shall be Land Sould at five Shillings p Acer or the Severall Creditors may have Land at five Shillings p Acre till they are paid If It dont Exceed the 150 Acres.
Atrue Record of the vote
Attes. John Southmayd Clerk.

Att the Same Meeting there was Chosen as Committe Lift John Hopkins John Richards and Thomas Hikcox to Represent the proprietors. and See what Debts are Duely Charged and Sign Notes to the measurers for their Mony Land.

A true Entry of the Vote

Attest. John Southmayd Clerk.

Att the Same Meeting It was by vote Agreed that where as there are Severall Persons that are behind hand In taking up their Lands that have been Allready Granted we do Give them till the Middle of Aprill next to take up their Lands. before we will go upon the Devision now Agreed upon and the Devision In the North West Corner of the bounds Shall be Laid out by that day and by the Committe formerly appointed for that work.

A true Record of the Vote

Attes. John Southmayd Clerk.

Att the Same Meting It was Agreed by their vote that the first Devision Now A Greed upon Shall be began to be taken up on the 16th day of Aprill next Ensueing the Date here of. that Is to Say he that Draws the first Lott Shall take up his proportion on the S^d Sixteenth of Aprill and he that draws the Second Lott his proportion on the Seventeenth of S^d Aprill and So Successively till the Last of May. and then to begin Again on the first of September following and go on In the Same Successive order till the Lott be finished. Excepting Sabboths and all publick dayes and Such dayes when the weather Is unsutable In the Judgement of the measurer Applied too and he whose turn falls on one of the Excepted dayes Shall Improve the Next proper day to take up his Land and he that neglects to take up his Alottment In his proper day as Above

Limited Shall Loose his turn So as not to hinder or obstruct any other man of his proper Day.

A true Record of the vote

Attest. John Southmayd Clerk.

The meeting adjurned to the twenty Seventh of this Instant November

Att A meeting of the Proprietors of Waterbury Meet by Adjurnment November 27. 1723.

Att the Meeting Thomas Clark was by vote Chose Ameasurer for the South East quarter of the bounds East of the River and south of farmington Road by the Bever pond.

A true Record Attes. John Southmayd Clerk.

Att the Same Meeting It was by vote Enacted that Lif^t. Standly Doc Porter and Thomas Hikcox Shall be A Committe perticularly to Settle the old Town platt Lotts. and So far as they Can Set out Each mans Lott. and where the Committe Can say where mens Lotts ly they may E[n]ter upon them. and the Lotts being Set out by the Committe the owners that bant Assigned to perticular Lotts May Agree Among them Selves About them In order to Get those Lots Recorded that are not yet upon Record and men may know where their Lands ly.

A true Record of the vote

Attest. John Southmayd Clerk.

Att the Same Meeting It was Enacted that the Committe Chosen to Inspect the dark Grants and records Lost where Lands have been Surveighed and bounds Lost the S^d Committe Shall take the best Information they Can Come att and then bring A Return As Near as they Can Come at to the proprietors that they may Give their Sanction on What Is done In

order to Get yr Land Settled and recorded and as to
Lands that have been Surveighed the owners of S^d
Land Shall bare the Charge of S^d Committe them Selves
and all Grants not Surveighed the Charge shall be
paid by the proprietors which Committe Shall be
ready wn Called by perticular persons or sent by the
proprietors.

A true Record of the vote

Attes. John Southmayd Clerk.

Att the Same Meeting there were two of the Committe that were formerly Chosen to Lay out the North
west Devision that obJected Against Attending on
that buisness Viz. Lif. Hickox and William Judd we
did by vote appoint John Scovill Ju^r and Thomas Porter
In their place with the remainder of the Committe for
that work.

A true Record of the Vote

Attes^d. John Southmayd Clerk.

The Meeting Adjurned till the 2^d tuseday In Aprill
Next.

At A meeting of the proprietors of Waterbury
Decem^r 16th 1723 where as there Is Sundry Lots
Laid out formerly with In the Bounds of the Land
Sequestred for A Devision at the North west part of
our bounds   tis Now Agreed upon that the Committy
appointed to Lay out S^d Sequestred Land According
as the Lott did Cast Each man Shall have full power
to Measure those Lands formerly Laid out and by
Agreement with the owners of S^d Lands bring them
Into as Good A form as may be for the Advantage of
the Lotts that are now to be Laid out.   Not moving
Any of S^d former Lotts from the place where they be

and s^d former Lotts are to have ordinary Measure. past
by A full vote

A true Record of the vote

Attes^d. John Southmayd Clerk.

A List and order of of the Lott that was Agreed upon
And Drawn for At A proprietors Meeting November.
26. 1723.

the Lott		the propriety
1	Thomas Brounson	40
2	Samuell Scott	40
3	Thomas Clark	40
4	the 2^d Proprietors Lott	40
5	Abraham Anddruss Se^r.	144
6	John Scovill. Ju^r.	40
7	John Richards Se^r.	144
8	Thomas Worner Se^r.	180
9	Joseph Hikcox Ju^r.	40
10	School Lott	270
11	Samuell Porter	40
12	Isaac Brounson Ju^r.	40
13	John Judd Ju^r.	40
14	Obadiah Scott	40
15	Thomas Handcox	180
16	Joseph Brounson	40
17	Richard Welton	40
18	Benjamin Bernes Ju^r.	40
19	John Brounson of Isaac	40
20	John Richason	40
21	John Southmayd	270
22	Thomas Anddruss	40
23	Samuell Worner of Thomas	40
24	the 3^d proprietors Lott	40
25	John Worner Se^r.	162

the Lott		the propriety
26	Nathaniell Richason	40
27	Daniell Porter Se[r].	171
28	George Scott Ju[r].	40
29	Stephen Hopkins	40
30	Obadiah Richards Ju[r].	40
31	Joseph Gailard Se[r].	144
32	Benjamin Richards	40
33	George Welton	40
34	Stephen Upson Se[r].	90
35	M[r] Jeremiah Peck	270
36	Abraham Anddruss Ju[r].	40
37	the first proprietors Lott	40
38	William Judd	40
39	John Carington	108
40	Lif[t]. John Hopkins	180
41	Ephraim Worner	40
42	Phillip Judd	144
43	Thomas Bernes	40
44	Thomas Newell	162
45	John Standly Se[r].	180
46	John Brounson Se[r].	144
47	Thomas Richason Se[r].	90
48	Cap[t]. Thomas Judd—Williams	180
49	Cap[t]. Thomas Judd. Jones	180
50	John Richards Ju[r].	40
51	Edmund Scott. Se[r].	180
52	John Judd Se[r].	180
53	Benjamin Worner Se[r].	40
54	Thomas Richards Se[r].	40
55	Stephen Upson Ju[r].	40
56	Samuell Hikcox Sen[r].	180
57	Jonathan Scott Se[r].	90
58	the 150[lb] propriety	150

the Lott		the propriety
59	Robert Scott	40
60	Thomas Upson	40
61	the 5th proprietors Lott	40
62	Stephen Welton	40
63	Lif^t Timothy Standly. Ba.	40
64	John Gailard	40
65	Abraham Anddruss. Cooper.	180
66	David Scott	40
67	Thomas Richason Ju^r.	40
68	John Newell	180
69	Jonathan Scott Ju^r.	40
70	Ebenezar Hikcox	40
71	Benjamin Worner Ju^r.	40
72	Joseph Hikcox Se^r.	108
73	John Bernes	40
74	George Scott Se^r.	40
75	Benjamin bernes. Se^r.	180
76	Obadiah Richards Se^r.	144
77	Isaac Brounson Se^r.	180
78	John Welton Se^r.	144
79	Joseph Lewis.	40
80	the 4th pro: Lott. w. Scot. J. Worner	40
81	Timothy Hopkins.	40
82	Richard Porter.	90
83	Daniell Worner.	108
84	Thomas Hikcox	40
85	Joseph Gailard Ju^r.	40
86	Ebenezar Richason	40
87	Edmun Scott Ju^r.	126
88	William Hikcox	40
89	Thomas Welton	40
90	Daniell Porter Ju^r.	40
91	John Hikcox	40

the Lott		the propriety
92	Samuell Standly	40
93	John Worner Se^r. B. Lott.	40
94	Timothy Stanly Original	180
95	the Sixth proprietors Lott.	40
96	Israell Richason.	40
97	John Scovill Se^r.	144
98	Thomas Judd Ju^r. Halls.	180
99	John We[l]ton Ju^r.	40
100	Ebenezar Brounson.	40

The proprietors of Waterbury Met on tuseday the 14th day of Aprill. 1724. According to Adjurnment. and finding no present buisness to do this meeting Is Adjurned to the Second tuseday In November Next.
Attes John Southmayd Clerk.

The proprietors of Waterbury Meet on tuse day the tenth of November 1724 According to Adjurnment and no business being before them the Meeting Was AdJurned to the Last tuseday In March Next.
Attes. John Southmayd Clerk.

A meeting of the proprietors of Waterbury According to AdJurnment March. 30. 1725. At the Same Meeting It was Agreed to Ad Jurn the Said meeting to the Last tuseday In November next.
Attes^t. John Southmayd Clerk.

November 30th 1725. A meeting of the proprietors. In Waterbury According to Adjurnment and No buisness being before them the meeting was adJurned to the Last tuse day In March Next.
John Southmayd Clerk.

March 29ᵗʰ 1726. the proprietors of Waterbury
Mett In Waterbury According to AdJurnment.
Att A proprietors Meeting Met by AdJurnment
March 29. 1726. It was by A vote Agreed that the
Committy appointed to Lay out the North west
Devision. Shall Go on With the work as they have
begun and finnish the Lott. as It is Divided to Each
proprietor. and If the Lotts dont take up the Land
the remainder Shall remain to the proprietors to be
Disposed of as the proprietors Shall Appoint. after
the Lott Is finished and If there bant Land Enough
for the Lotts to be Laid In. the Remaining Lotts
may be taken up In Any of our Other undivided Lands
as we do our Other Devisions.

Att the Same Meeting Lift Hikcox the measurer In
the North East quarter of the bounds was by vote put
out from being Measurer.

Att the Same Meeting John Judd Was Chosen
Measurer for the North East quarter of the bounds.

Att the Same Meeting It was Enquired wheither
we would now Go on Another Devision Voted In the
Negative.

At the Same Meeting John Judd was appointed one
of the Committe In the Room of John Scovill Juʳ. and
James Porter In the Room of Thoˢ. Porter to Lay out
the Lotts In the North west Devision. the Meeting
AdJurned to the Last Tuseday In November Next.

Att A meeting of the proprietors of Waterbury Mett
by AdJurnment November 29. 1726. the Proprietors
Looking upon A vote passed November 27. 1722. where
the proprietors made Six forty pound proprieties
which were to ly for the Proprietors use. we did by A

vote Agree and Conclude that those Six Proprietors Lotts Shall have all the Devisions that were formerly made to the forty pound proprieties Viz. the 38 Acres the 30 Acres the 55 Acres the Devision in the Northwest Devision the 40 Acre Devision Drawn for In 1723. Nov. 26. and Aproportion In All After Devisions with In the township according to A forty pound propriety. only they Shall not take the Eight Acres In the Town Sequester as the Bacheldors did.

A true Record Attes. John Southmayd Clerk.

Att the Same meeting It appearing that there were four of the Six proprietors Lotts that were not disposed of. we did by Avote Agree that the four proprietors Lotts that the proprietors have yet In their hands Shall be disposed of by A Committy and the mony Laid out to the building of Ameetinghouse to be Erected In Waterbury on the Spot that was Agreed up on at A Town meeting In Waterbury Jan. 7th 1722/3

A true Record Attest. John Southmayd Clerk.

November 29th 1726.

Att the Same Meeting Lif. William Hikcox and William Judd and Timothy Hopkins were Chosen A Committe whom we do Impower to sell the Above S^d four proprietors Lotts and give Deeds there of. to the Grantees and take the money and put It Into the hands of the Committe that Shall be Chosen by the Town to order the Affair of building A meeting hous as Is above Expressed

A true Record Attes^d John Southmayd Clerk.

Att the Same Meeting It was by A vote Agreed that If the Committy for the old town plat Lotts Cant find all the old town platt Lotts for all the orginal proprietors those that are wanting may have Liberty to take them up in the undivided Lands.

Atrue Record Attes. John Southmayd Clerk.

Att the Same Meeting It was by Avote Agreed that we will Go upon A Nother Devision of our out Lands of fifty Acres on A fifty pound propriety and So proportionably for Greater or lesser proprieties which Devision shall be Regulated Next proprietors Meeting.

A true Record Attes. John Southmayd Clerk

the Meeting Ad Jurned to the Second tuse day In March Next.

Att A meeting of the proprietors of Waterbury Met by adJurnment. March 13. 1727.

At the Same meeting the proprietors made Choise of John Brounson Ju^r. Ameasurer In the north west Quarter of the Bounds. and Serg^t. Judd to be helpfull to him In Difficult Cases and Call^d.

A true Record Attest John Southmayd Clerk.

Att the Same meeting the proprietors made Choise of Deacon Judd Moderator to Act with Liff Hopkins or Alone Incase of his Absence.

Atrue Record Attes. John Southmayd Clerk.

Att the Same Meeting the proprietors made Choise of Will Judd John Southmayd and John Brounson to Look over the Imperfect Surveighs Left by Serg^t Scovill and fit them for the Record

A true Record Attest. John Southmayd Clerk.

Att the Same meeting the proprietors did by vote Agree that we will now prepare and draw A Lott for the Lott Agreed upon the Last meeting.

Attes. John Southmayd Clerk.

Att the Same meeting It was by Vote Agreed that the Lott now drawn for Shall beregulated as the Lott was that was Agreed and Drawn for Novem 26. 1723. Excepting the time of beginning to Lay out the Lott.

Att. John Southmayd Clerk.

Att the Same Meeting It was by vote Agreed that the Lott now drawn for Shall begin to be Laid out the first Lott on the first working day In September next. and So to Hold on In Course till the middle of November next. and then to Scease till the first of march And then to begin Again And hold on till the Lott be finneshed.—

A. T. R.   Attes: John Southmayd Clerk.

Att the Same Meeting Lif. Timothy Standly Declareing before the proprietors that If they would quietly resign A Bacheldors Lott to Him. belonging to his original Propriety which he had been keept out of he would make Sale of It and dedicate the money there of to the building the meeting house we are now About building where upon the proprietors did by their vote Declare that they did resighn the Above S^d propriety to the Said Lift Timothy Standly he dedicateing of It to the use Above S^d.

A. T. R.   Attes. John Southmayd Clerk.

Att the Same Meeting the proprietors did by vote Agree that the Lott now drawn Shall In order be put on Record.

A. T. R.   Att. John Southmayd Clerk.

Att the Same meeting the proprietors voted that there Shall be four Acres more Added to A piece of Land on the Side of Long hill formerly Laid to the ministry but not Recorded that the whole may be Returned to Record.

Attes. John Southmayd Clerk.

The proprietors Meeting AdJurned to the 2^d tuse day In March Next.

A List of the Lott drawn for March 13th 1727. and the order In Which It was drawn.

Lott

1 Joseph Gailard Ju^r.
2 Benjamin Richards
3 Benjamin Bernes Ju^r.
4 John Welton Se^r.
5 Benjamin Worner Ju^r.
6 John Gailard
7 John Welton Ju^r.
8 John Worner Se^r. Bacheldor Lot.
9 Isaac Brounson Se^r.
10 Thomas Hikcox
11 John Newel
12 Timothy Hopkins
13 John Richard Ju^r.
14 John Stanly Se^r.
15 Timothy Stanly Original
16 the first proprietors Lott.
17 Thomas Richard Se^r.
18 George Welton.
19 George Scott Se^r.
20 M^r. Jeremiah Peck.
21 Benjamin Worner Se^r.
22 Robert Scott.
23 Stephen Welton
24 Thomas Worner se^r.
25 Benjamin Bernes Se^r.
26 Samuel Worner of Thomas
27 School Lott.
28 John Judd Se^r.
29 John Judd Ju^r.
30 Isaac Brounson Ju^r
31 John Richason
32 John Brounson of Isaac
33 Thomas Richason Se^r.
34 John Carington.
35 Obadiah Richards Se^r.
36 John Southmayd.
37 Phillip Judd.
38 the 4th Proprietors Lott.

Lott

39 John Brounson Se^r.
40 Abraham Andruss Cooper.
41 Thomas Judd Ju^r. Halls.
42 Joseph Brounson.
43 Rich = ard Porter
44 Ephraim Worner.
45 Stephen Hopkins.
46 Thomas Richason Ju^r.
47 David Scott.
48 Nathaniel Richason
49 Thomas Newel
50 Israel Richason
51 the Sixth proprietors Lott.
52 Daniel Porter Se^r.
53 Jonathan Scott Se^r.
54 William Hikcox.
55 Thomas Bernes
56 John Scovill Ju^r.
57 Joseph Lewis
58 Ebenezar Hikcox
59 the 5th proprietors Lott
60 Richard Welton
61 Daniel Porter Ju^r.
62 Jonathan Scott Ju^r.
63 Samuel Porter
64 John Bernes
65 Samuel Stanly
66 Samuel Scott
67 Abraham Anddruss Se^r.
68 Thomas Upson
69 Cap Thomas Judd Jones
70 Samuel Hikcox Se^r.
71 Thomas Welton
72 John Scovill Se^r.
73 Thomas Brounson
74 Joseph Hikcox Se^r.
75 William Judd.
76 Cap Thoms Judd William
77 Edmund Scott Ju^r.

Lott

78 | Thomas Handcox
79 | the third proprietor Lott.
80 | Stephen Upson Ju^r.
81 | Stephen Upson Se^r.
82 | George Scott Ju^r.
83 | Lif John Hopkins
84 | Abraham Anddruss Ju^r.
85 | Edmund Scott Se^r.
86 | John Worner Se^r.
87 | the Second proprietor lott
88 | John Hikcox
89 | Thomas Clark

Lott

90 | Joseph Gailard Se^r.
91 | Lif Timothy Stanly B. Lott
92 | Thomas Anddruss.
93 | 150^lb propriety.
94 | Ebenezar Brounson.
95 | Obadiah Richards Ju^r.
96 | Daneil Worner.
97 | Obadiah Scott.
98 | John Richards Se^r.
99 | Joseph Hikcox Ju^r.
100 | Ebenezar Richason

the proprietors of Waterbury Meett According to AdJurnment In Waterbury March 12th. 1728.

Att the Same Meeting of the Proprietors It Appearing to them that George Scott had taken up four Acres of Land that was formerly Granted to Israel Richason Lying between the pine Hole and the Common fence Granted December. 17th 1696. they did by vote Agree that Israel Richasons Heirs might have Liberty to take up four Acres In Lew of It. In the Sequester Land provided Capt Judd one of the Guardians Engaging for him self and Successors. that the Heirs Shall never make Any other Demands on the proprietors nor Any Other person for the Above S^d grant of four Acres at pine hole and In Seting his hand to this Grant Oblidge him Self there too Signed In presence of the proprietors Thomas Judd. and John Southmayd Clerk.

Atrue Record Attes. John Southmayd Clerk.

Att the Same Meeting It appearing to the proprietors that there was A Difficulty About the up River Devision. It was Concluded that one Hundred pound propriety In that Devision Should have Six acres and

So proportionally for greater or lesser proprieties and No more.

Atrue Record of the vote Attes.

John Southmayd Clerk.

Att the Same Meeting they made Choise of Capt Thomas Judd A Committe man with Isaac Brounson and Joseph Lewis who were formerly appointed A Committe to Inspect Dark and Large Grants and Make Areturn to the proprietors.

Atrue Record Attest John Southmayd Clerk.

Att the Same Meeting It being Desired of the Proprietors to Resolve wheither Aformer Measurer where there Is Another Chosen In his Room has power to Lay out Land and the Clark oblidged if Any Such Should presume to Lay out. oblidged to record It. resolved In the Negative.

Attest John Southmayd Clerk.

Att the Same meeting upon the request of Deacon Thomas Hikcox with respect to A grant of four Acres on the west Side of Caringtons Brook granted March 28 1694/5 Desiring that on relinquishing It. he might have liberty to take It Else where by his own Land In the Sequester. the proprietors Granted him four Acres to be taken up by his own Land In the Sequester. not prejudishing former Grants. Provided A relinquishment be signed by the S^d Hikcox.

I Thomas Hikcox do hereby relinquish my Right to A grant of four Acres Granted March. 28th 1694/5. lying on the west Side Caringtons Brook. witness my Hand.

Thomas Hikcox.

Signed In presence of the proprietors. and John Southmayd Clerk.

Att the Same Meeting the proprietors made Choise

of William Judd A measurer to Lay out Land In the North west quarter of the Bounds In the Room of John Brounson.

The Meeting Adjurned to the Last tuse day In May Next.

The Proprietors of Waterbury Meet According to AdJurnment on the Last tuse day In May 1728. and No business appearing the meeting was adJurned to the Last Tuesday In November Next.

Att A Meeting of the proprietors of Waterbury Mett by Legal Worning In Waterbury March 11ᵗʰ. 1730.
then Capᵗ. Judd. and Mʳ Isaac Brounson were Chosen Moderators to Lead In the proprietors Meeting.

Att the Same Meeting It was Agreed that our proprietors Meeting Shall be Continued and Worned by Adjurnment.

Att the Same Meeting William Judd. Docʳ Ephraim Worner. and Deacon Clark were Chosen A Committe to Inspect that there be No Incroachment on proprietors Land or that owned by perticular persons.

Att A meeting of the proprietors. March 11ᵗʰ 1730.

Att the Same Meeting It was by A vote A Greed that there Shall be A Rate Levyed on the present proprietors of A half penny on the pound.

Att the Same Meeting the proprietors Made Choise of the former Committe William Judd Capᵗ Worner and Deacon Clark. A Committe to Agree with perticular persons where high Wayes run through their Lands and to Say what Recompence they Shall have for the Dammage Done them and the Committe A Greeing with the persons Damnified and Making

Return to the proprietors their Agreement Shall be Sufficient to the Holding the Lands Set out to them for A Recompence.

Att the Same Meeting the proprietors by vote Agreed and Appointed their former Committe Cap Tho Judd. Isaac Brounson and Joseph Lewis that were to Inspect the dark Grant. and Antient Grants Also to Surveigh them on the Charge of those persons whom the Grants belong unto.

Att the Same Meeting the proprietors by vote Agreed. that what the Committe to Look After. And Settle the old Town platt Lotts. did In thatt Matter Shall be put on Record. and those of the Original proprietors that want y^r Lotts y^r Shall have their Eight Acres In Some place in the undivided Land.

att the Same meeting It was Voted that there Should be A Record made of the Return of the Division In the North west Quarter. with the number of Acres belonging to Each Lott as presented by the Committe.

Att the Same Meeting the proprietors appointed Thomas Barnes Collector for the proprietors Rates now Granted.

Att the Same Meeting the proprietors Made Choise of Timothy Hopkins A William Judd to take Advice About the line between farmington and us And prosecute the Same In the Law If need be for the Setling of S^d Line.

Att the Same Meeting the proprietors Made Choise of James Porter Measurer on the west side of the River. with William Judd to Measure Land With S^d Judd. or with out him as he Shall be Called.

Att the Same Meeting It was by vote Agreed and Concluded that they Look upon John Standlies Ju^r. Right to be Good to A Bacheldor Lott and he ought

to have Anote for his Land to be Laid out and he
Engaged. that the Proprietors Might have the Eight
Acres In the Sequester to be Desposed by them as they
See Cause.

Att the Same Meeting the meeting was AdJurned
to the Last Tuseday In Aprill.

A list of the Lott In the North west Quarter of the
Bounds and the Number of Acres belonging to Each
Man In the Division.

Lott	the proprietors Names.	Acres	Rood	Rods
1	Daniel Porter Ju\u207f.	16	00	20
2	William Hikcox	16	00	20
3	Joseph Hikcox	43	01	14
4	John Hikcox	16	00	20
5	Benjamin Richards	16	00	20
6	Samuel Hikcox Se\u207f.	72	02	10
7	Lieu\u1d57. John Hopkins	72	02	10
8	Joseph Gailard Ju\u207f.	16	00	20
9	John Brounson of Isaac	16	00	20
10	John Judd Ju\u207f.	16	00	20
11	Jonathan Scott Ju\u207f.	16	00	20
12	Robert Scott	16	00	20
	Highway			
13	Edmund Scott Ju\u207f.	50	03	01
14	Thomas Worner	72	02	10
15	Abraham Anddrus or M\u207f Whittlesey	72	02	10
16	Isaac Brounson Se\u207f.	72	02	10
	Highway			
17	David Scott	16	00	20
18	Obadiah Scott	16	00	20
19	Stephen Upon Se\u207f.	36	01	05
20	Joseph Hikcox Ju\u207f.	16	00	20
21	Benjamin Worner Se\u207f.	16	00	20
22	John Worner Se\u207f.	65	01	09
	Highway			
23	John Stanly Se\u207f	72	02	10
24	Thomas Judd Ju\u207f. M\u207f Halls	72	02	10
25	Edmund Scott Se\u207f.	72	02	10
	Highway			

Lott	the Proprietors Names.	Acres	Rood	Rods
26	Timothy Hopkins	16	00	20
27	Thomas Welton	16	00	20
28	Richard Porter	36	01	05
29	Stephen Welton	16	00	20
30	George Scott x	16	00	20
31	Samuel Stanly	16	00	20
32	John Scovill Ju^r.	16	00	20
33	Phillip Judd	64	01	08
	Highway			
34	John Carington	43	01	14
35	the first Proprietors Lott	16	00	20
36	the Second Proprietors Lott	16	00	20
37	Stephen Hopkins	16	00	20
38	Benjamin Barns Se^r. Uper Lot	72	02	10
39	Daniel Worner	43	01	14
40	John Brounson Se^r.	64	01	08
41	Thomas Clark	16	00	20
42	John Barns	16	00	20
43	Ebenezar Hikcox	16	00	20
44	Capt. Thomas Judds. Williams	72	02	10
45	School Lott	108	03	15
	Highway			
46	Nathaniel Richason	16	00	20
47	George Scott Ju^r.	16	00	20
48	Lieu^t. Timothy Stanly Original	72	02	10
49	Cap Thomas Judd Jones	72	02	10
	Highway			
50	Ebenezar Richason	16	00	20
51	Abraham Anddruss Ju^r.	16	00	20
52	Thomas Richason Se^r.	36	01	05
53	Obadiah Richards Ju^r.	16	00	20
54	Joseph Lewis	16	00	20
55	Thomas Handcox	72	02	10
	Highway			
56	Mr Jeremiah Peck	108	03	15
57	John Welton Se^r.	64	01	08
	Highway			
58	William Judd	16	00	20
59	John Gailard	16	00	20
60	Ebenezar Brounson	16	00	20
61	John Richason	16	00	20
62	Joseph Gailard Se^r.	64	01	08

Lott	the Proprietors Names.	Acres	Rood	Rods
63	Daniel Porter Se[r].	68	03	29
	Highway			
64	the fifth Proprietors Lott. M. B.	16	00	20
65	Stephen Upson Ju[r].	16	00	20
66	Samuel Porter	16	00	20
67	John Scovill Se[r].	64	01	08
68	John Richards	64	01	08
69	Thomas Richards Se[r].	16	00	20
70	Thomas Bernes	16	00	20
71	John Judd Se[r].	72	02	10
72	Abraham Anddrus Se[r].	64	01	08
73	Benjamin Worner Ju[r].	16	00	20
74	John Welton Ju[r].	16	00	20
	Highway			
75	Thomas Hikcox	16	00	20
76	the fourth Proprietors Lott	16	00	20
77	John Southmayd	108	03	15
78	Lieu[t]. Timothy Stanly. B. Lott	16	00	20
	Highway			
79	Richard Welton	16	00	20
80	Sam[ll] Worner of Thomas	16	00	20
81	Joseph Brounson	16	00	20
82	George Welton	16	00	20
83	Thomas Newel	65	01	09
84	Thomas Upson	16	00	20
85	Isaac Brounson Ju[r].	16	00	20
86	150[lb] propriety	60	01	35
	Highway			
87	Israel Richason	16	00	20
88	Samuel Scott of Edmund	16	00	20
89	Thomas Anddruss	16	00	20
90	Thomas Richason Ju[r].	16	00	20
91	John Richards Ju[r].	16	00	20
92	Thom Brounson	16	00	20
93	Jonathan Scott Se[r].	36	01	05
94	John Newel	72	02	10
	Highway			
95	Ephraim Worner	16	00	20
96	Benjamin Barns Ju[r].	16	00	20
97	the Third Proprietors Lott	16	00	20
98	Obadiah Richards Se[r].	64	01	08
99	John Worner Se[r]. Bacheldor Lott	16	00	20
100	the Sixth Proprietors Lott	16	00	20

This list of the Lott In the North west Division seting forth Each mans Proportion In that Division Made by Order of the proprietors as may be seen by their act att their meeting M a r c h 11th 1730 and Entered by John Southmayd Clerk A true Record of the Original as Attests John Southmayd Clerk.

A List of the House Lotts on the Old Town Platt Set out by A Committee. Lieut. Timothy Stanly Doctor Daniel Porter Se^r And Deacon Thomas Hikcox. We began on the west teer att the North End and Found as follows

first. John Brounsons Lott.
Second. Edmund Scotts Lott.
third. Isaac Brounsons Lott.
fourth. Sam^{ll} Hikcox Se^r. Lott.
fifth. Doctor Porters Lott.
Sixth. A Great Lott.
Seventh. A Great Lott.
Eight. John Warners Lott.
then an Eight Rod Highway; South of Warners Lott. that Runs East and West. or as the Lotts ly.
Ninth Thomas Richasons Lott.
tenth Joseph Hikcox Lott.
Eleventh. L. Timothy Stanlies Lott.
twelfh. John Newells Lott.
thirteenth. Benjamin Joneses Lott.
fourteenth L. John Stanlies Lott.
fifteenth Deacon Judds Lott.
sixteenth John Hopkins Lott.
then we began Att the South End of the East teer and found
first. Deacon Judds Lott.

Second David Carpenters Lott.
third Abraham Anddruss Lott.
fourth. Lieut. Judds Lott.
fifth. Edmund Scott Se^r. Lott.
Sixth. Lieut Timothy Stanlies Lott.
Seventh. Abraham Anddruss Cooper Lott.
Eight. Benjamin Barns Lott.
Ninth. Thomas Newels Lott.
then Eight Rods Highway to Run East. and West, or as the Lotts Ly
tenth. Obadiah Richards Lott.
Eleventh Thomas Worners Lott.
twelfth John Scovills Lott.
thirteenth. John Carington's Lott.
fourteenth John Weltons Lott.
fifteenth. Daniel Worner's Lott.
Sixteenth. Thomas Judd Lott.
the Severall Lotts In the west teer but. East on Highway.
the Severall Lotts In the East teer but West on High way.

Daniel Porter
found by the   Thomas Hikcox
Committe.   His
Timothy + Stanly
mark

this Return of the Committe
Entred by or Der of the Proprie-

tors att their meeting. as may be
Seen by their Act March. 11.
1730. and Entered by
John Southmayd Clerk.
A true Record of the Return
as attests.
John Southmayd Clerk.

Att A meeting of the proprietors of Waterbury Mett
According to Adjurnment. Aprill. 28th 1730. Att the
Same the proprietors Made Choise of Mr Isaac Brounson and Sergt Joseph Lewis. A Committe to meet
with A Committe from Woodbury to Settle and Make
Monuments According to Law. In the line between
us. from the black oak tree In the line 80 Rods East
of Quassapaug pond to the South west Corner of our
bounds which Is Agreed to be A Strait line.

the Meeting AdJurned to the second tuseday In
December Next.

the proprietors Meet According to AdJurnment and
the proprietors Adjurned the meeting to the first
monday of February Next. which will be In the year.
1731.

The proprietors Met According to Adjurnment
Feb. 1. 1731. And then It was by Vote Agreed that
if the Committe to Lay out the Lotts In the North
west Division dont do the Work and prepare It to be
Laid before the proprietors by the third Monday In
may Next. that then the Committe to Sign Notes for
Land to pay for the work Shall have No power to sign
Any Notes to Any of them With out Further order
from the proprietors.

Att the Same Meeting It was Agreed that Such

Survayes of high wayes as Are Returned to be Accepted by the proprietors. And Accepted by them the proprietors to pay the Charge.

Att the Same Meeting the high way Laid out from Isaac Medow Barrs to Nickolses and to Woodbury bounds by William Judd and James Porter Accepted by the proprietors and Ordered to be Entred.

Waterbury Feb. 1. 1731.

Att the Same Meeting the proprietors by Vote Appointed A Committe to find out the propriety belonging to Each man and make A Rate as Granted on the proprietors and for A Committe John Southmayd Seg^t Joseph Lewis and Capt. William Judd. Appointed.

Att the Same Meeting Thomas Barns the former proprietors Collector Refuseing the Work, Ephraim Bissell was Chosen proprietors Collector to Gather the proprietors Rate Granted In March 1730.

Att the Same Meeting A Committe was made Choise of to Lay out needfull High wayes In the proprietors Land and Say what Allowance men Shall have for Dammage Done by High wayes. And for A Committe. Capt William Hikcox Capt William Judd. And Deacon Clark were Chosen.

Att the Same Meeting Capt William Hikcox was put Into the Same power with Respect to High wayes that Doc Worner Had.

The meeting by Vote Adjurned to the third Monday In May Next.

The Meeting Meet According to AdJurnment on the third monday of may 1731. And No buisness. Appearing the meating Adjurned to the Second Tuse day In December Next.

The Proprietors Meet According to AdJurnment on the Second Tuseday In December 1731. and No buisness Appearing the Meeting adJourned to the Second Tuseday In February Next.

The Proprietors of Waterbury Meet According to Adjurnment on the Second Tuseday of February. 1731/2. And No buisness Appearing the meeting Adjourned to the Second Tuseday of Aprill Next.

Att A proprietors Meeting Meet by Adjournment In Waterbury Aprill. 11th 1732. It Was Agreed by Vote that Capt. William Judd And Capt Timothy Hopkins Dean. Thomas Clark be A Committe to Confer With Farmington A bout the Line betwixt them and us and Shall Have Full power to A Gree And Fully Settle the line betwixt them and us and Doctor Ephraim Worner Is Aded to the Former Committe.

Att the Same Meeting the proprietors Chose Sergt Thomas Brounson and John Judd and Benjamin Worner A Committe to Exchange one Acre And Sixty Rods of Land with Robert Johnson He giving A Quit Claim to the proprietors.

Att the Same Meeting It was Acted that If Doc. Daniel Porter Quit His Right to A Certain peice of Land Att the Spectacle ponds that was his fathers to the proprietors he Shall Have Liberty to take So much Land In the Sequestred Land as Is In the Afore Sd Tract of Land where It Sutes him best And be Laid out by Deacon Thomas Clark or John Judd.

Att the Same Meeting It was Agreed by Vote. That Dean Thomas Clark With the Town Clerk Shall be A Committe to Search Docr Ephraim Worners

Records to Know Wheither he Has had All His Land According to His propriety or purchase and If he has not So much Laid out as He Has A Right too then to Have Anote for the Remainder. And the Same Committe are to Consider Any persons under the like Scir cum stances With S^d Worner.

Att the Same Meeting It was Voted that Apent Road. Shall be through the Mad medows up to the Common fence and So to the Cuntry Road to Juds Meadow Laid out by the Committe Chose by the proprietors. A true Record of the Act of the Meeting In Aprill 11. 1732.

Attest. John Southmayd Clerk.

The Meeting Adjourned to the Last tuseday of December Next Ensueing.

Att the Meeting of the proprietors In Waterbury Mett by Adjournment December 26th 1732. And no buiness Done. but the Meeting Adjourned to the Second Tuseday In In February Next.

A meeting of the proprietors of Waterbury Met by Adjournment the Second tuseday of February 1732/3. the Meeting opened and but Afew people of the proprietors there the Meeting adjourned for Half an hour. and then Met According to Adjournment. and then Voted that they would Go upon A Division of their Sequestred Lands to be Divided According to Each mans Propriety.

Att the Same Meeting there was made Choise of A Committe to Lay out the Sequestred Land and High wayes. Capt Timothy Hopkins Lieu^t Sam^{ll} Hikcox. Cap. wi^{ll} Judd.

Att the Same Meeting the proprietors by their Vote

Declare that In the Laying out of the Sequester Land the Comitte Appointed to that work Shall have power to Lay out all Necessary And Conveniant High wayes to be Left to the Descretion of the Committe where the high wayes Shall be and How wide. only they Shall not Exceed fifteen Rods In Any place Except where It is Exceeding Difficult passing and wher It passes through mens Land not to Exceed four Rods.

the Meeting Adjourned to the 14th Day of this Instant February.

Att the Same Meeting It was Voted that In the Division of the Sequestred Land Itt Shall be Laid out Lott by Lott Succesively beginning Att A Certain place In the Sequester as Shall be Agreed upon till Every Man has His Lott According to propriety And the Committe In Laying out Have power to Size the Land.

Daniel Porter Entred His protest Against the first vote of the Second Days Meeting and Desired to Have His protest Entred.

Att the Same Meeting the proprietors by their Vote Declare that In Dividing of the Sequester Land the teers to be Laid out Shall Run North and South and to be Laid out In four teers And A highway between Every teer. and to begin att the North End of the East teer with the first Lott and to Run southward with the Lotts Successively till that teer be out and then to Run up with the Lott In the Second teer and Down In the Third teer and then Northward In the fourth teer till Every man Has his Lott Accord to Draught.

Att the Same Meeting. there was A Committe Appointed to Search the Records and to find out what Lands were Laid out with In the Sequester Land that have been now Agreed upon to be Divided and the proprietors Voted for A Committe the Town Clerk and Capt. William Judd.

Att the Same Meeting Avote for the Lott being prepared James Porter by Vote was Chosen to Draw the Lott. and then the Lott Drawn.

Att the Same Meeting It was Voted that the Committe to Lay out the Sequester Land Shall Go upon the Work by the Middle of Next March.

Att the Same Meeting the proprietors Voted that the Lott Drawn Shall be put on Record.

The Meeting Adjourned to the Second Tuseday In March Next to Meet in the Meeting House att Eight A Clock In the Morning.

A true Entry of the Votes of the proprietors Att their Meeting In Waterbury February 13th and Feb. 14th as Attests. John Southmayd Clerk.

The order of the Lott In the Sequester Land as It was Drawn att Att Aproprietors Meeting In Waterbury Feb. 14. 1732/3. and Ordered to be entred.

1	Thomas Brounsons	9	Ebenezar Brounson
2	Benjamin Barns Ju^r.	10	Phillip Judd.
3	Timothy Stanlys Bach: Lott	11	John Hikcox
4	Joseph Gailard Se^r.	12	Jonathan Scott Ju^r.
5	John Judd Ju^r.	13	Benjamin Worner Ju^r.
6	Obadiah Scott.	14	Isaac Brounson Ju^r.
7	Thos. Richards Se^r.	15	Richard Welton.
8	Sam^{ll} Worner of Tho.	16	Stephen Hopkins.
		17	Thos Barns.

10

18	Capt Tho Judd William	59	John Southmayd.
19	Thomas Richason Ju^r.	60	Isaac Brounson Se^r.
20	Benjamin Barns Se^r.	61	Joseph Hikcox Ju^r.
21	Edmund Scott Ju^r.	62	John Barns.
22	third Proprietor Lott.	63	Abraham Anddruss Se^r.
23	George Scott Ju^r.	64	Joseph Lewis.
24	M^{r}Jeremiah Peck.	65	John Brounson of Isaac.
25	Cap Thomas Judd.	66	Timothy Hopkins.
26	Robert Scott.	67	John Newel.
27	George Welton	68	George Scott Ju^r.
28	Edmund Scott Se^r.	69	Daniel Porter Ju^r.
29	Stephen Upson Ju^r.	70	John Richards Se^r.
30	Stephen Welton.	71	John Carington
31	Samuel Stanly	72	Abraham Anddruss Ju^r
32	David Scott.	73	Nathaniel Richason
33	John Judd Se^r.	74	John Stanly Se^r.
34	Doc^r. Ephraim Worner.	75	Obadiah Richards Se^r.
35	William Hikcox.	76	Shool Lott.
36	Abraham Anddruss. Cooper.	77	Joseph Gailard Ju^r.
37*	John Brounson Se^r.	78	150^{lb} Propriety.
38	Thomas Hikcox.	79	Samuel Porter.
39	Thos Judd Halls.	80	John Scovill Ju^r.
40	Benjamin Richards.	81	Israel Richason.
41	John Hopkins.	82	Fifth Proprietors Lott.
42	Thomas Anddruss.	83	Daniel Worner
43	John Richason	84	Joseph Brounson
44	Thomas Clark.	85	John Richards Ju^r.
45	John Worners B. Lott	86	Obadiah Richards Ju^r.
46	Daniel Porter Se^r.	87	Thomas Welton
47	Jonathan Scott Se^r.	88	John Scovill Se^r.
48	the forth Pro. Lott. to Worner and Scott.	89	Stephen Upson Se^r.
		90	John Welton se^r.
49	Timothy Stanly Orig:	91	Thomas Newel.
50	Thos Worner Se^r.	92	Benjamin Worner Se^r.
51	the Sixth Proprietors Lott.	93	the Second Pro: Lott.
52	Samuel Scott.	94	John Worner Se^r.
53	Thomas Richason S^{er}.	95	Ebenezar Richason
54	Samuel Hikcox Se^r.	96	John Welton Ju^i.
55	Richard Porter.	97	John Gailard
56	William Judd. B. L.	98	Ebenezar Hikcox
57	Joseph Hikcox Se^r.	99	the fifth Pro. Lott.
58	Thomas Hikcox	100	Thomas Upson.

A proprietors Meeting In Waterbury Mett by Ad-Journment. March. 13th 1733.

the Meeting opened and then AdJourned for one Hour. and then Mett Again according to Ad Journment. Att which Meeting the proprietors Reconsidered their Vote past Last February with Respect to Dividing their Sequester Land and finding It Likely to be Very prejudicial to the Town to Make Such a Division and go on there with besides the thing Appearing Very Impracticable as to Sizeing therefore Concluded by their Votes to Let that Division Fall and by their vote Do Make Voide the Same.

Att the Same Meeting It was by Vote Agreed that In the North west Quarter of the bounds there Shall be Sequestred one Mile and Half North from the Center of the Society that Shall there be Allowed. and A mile and Half west and A mile and Half East and a mile and Half South all from the Center. all the Land Within that Compass not Laid out be Sequestred to ly for the Towns use. but not to prejudice any former Grants or Divisions not yet Laid out and to be under the Same Regulation with the Sequester Land on the East Side of the Town (Except that men Shant have liberty to Lay out any of their Divisions not yet Laid out. In the Eldest Sequester) and Each of these Sequesters to undivided one As Long as the Other.

Att the Same Meeting It being Laid before the proprietors that there was A Grant Granted to John Richason Deceased of four or five Acres of Land. Att Woster swamp Att the West End of His Fathers Lott which Is taken up by David Scott the proprietors Gave the Heirs that the Grant Is Destributed unto Liberty to take up the Land In Any of the undivided Land. the Meeting Addjourned to the Second Tuseday In November Next.

A true Record of the Acts of the metting Entred and Attested by John Southmayd Clerk.

Att A meeting of the proprietors In Waterbury Met by AdJournment the Second Tuseday In November According to former AdJournment And the Meeting Further Adjourned to the second Tuseday In Aprill Next.

Att A meeting of the proprietors. In Waterbury Met by Adjournment On the Second Tuseday In Aprill. 1734. And by Vote the Meeting Adjourned for one Houre. And Meet Again According to the AdJournment And by A Vote It was Acted that the Doings of the Committee for laying out the Northwest Division as It Is Returned Shall be Entred on Record.

Whereas It Appeared to the proprietors that Many times there Arose A Considerable Difficulty. by Reson of the Measurers Laying out Land to perticular persons before the note on Which the Land to be Laid out and was to be Indorsed was produced It was by the Vote of the proprietors Enacted that no measurers Shall Lay out Any Land to Any person till he Lay before the measurer the note on which the Land Is to be Indorsed Signifying that he has Land to Lay out and So much as he Desires to be Laid out. that It may be Immediately Indorsed.

Att the Same Meeting It was Voted that Capt. William Judd Shall be Limited to Lay out Land In the Northwest Quarter North of Woodbury Road and West of our River And James Porter In the Southwest Quarter South of Woodbury Road and West of our River.

Where as I Thomas Porter have bought of Joseph Gailard A grant Att Muddy Gutter of ten Acres Granted to Joseph Gailard Se^r. January 7th 1705/6. which Spot Is Allready Survayed to Other persons upon the proprietors Granting me Liberty to take It Else Where In the undivided Land. Ido by these presents resign my Right In the Spott on Which the Grant Was Made as Witness my hand In the presence of the proprietors Att their Meeting. the 10 Acres Laidout to Eb. Baldwin

Thomas Porter.

Witnesses. Isaac Brounson
Thomas Judd

Att the Same Meeting Capt. William Judd was Impowered to make Sale of the Eight Acres In the Sequester y^t John Stanly Gave to the Meeting house In Waterbury and put It In to the hands of the Committes hands who Carry on the Work of the Meeting House to be Applyed to S^d use.

Att the Same Meeting upon the request of Stephen Hopkins Concerning Agrant Made to Samuel Hikcox of Eight Acres Eastward of Judds Meadow he relinquishing five Acres att Chesnut Hill Meadow And two Acres of Upland And It Appearing that the Eight Acres Att S^d place are taken up they Voted the Heirs of S^d Hikcox or their Assigns. Shall have Liberty to take up Said Eight Acres Joyning to S^d Hopkins Land provided that Sd Hikcox Heirs Quit their Right to the Above S^d Seven Acres In form unto the proprietors and be Att the Charge.

the Meeting by Vote AdJourned to the first Tuseday In October to Consider About High ways.

I the Subscriber Do by these presents. Relinquish and Resign all the Right Title Intrest. In five Acres att Chesnutt Hill Meadow. and Two Acres of up Land. Granted to my Honoured father as Appears on Record.

Haveing Had the Eight Acres. Granted In lue of It and Sould to Stephen Hopkins. Do there fore Resign the Above S^d 5 and two Acres unto the proprietors of Waterbury to be Desposed of by them as they See Cause In Witness Where of I have here unto Set my Hand the Ninth of December. 1734:

Gideon Hikcox.

In presence of Witnesses.
Jn°. Southmayd.
Chileab Brainerd

Att A meeting of the Proprietors of Waterbury Meet In Waterbury by A worning Given According to Law by A warrant Signed by the Authority In Waterbury and Summoned to Meet on the 30th of March 1736. to Consider About Highwayes and Do Some thing About Incroach ments upon proprietors Land and Wheither It bant Needfull to make Some Division of the Land And Other business &c

Att the Meeting. Mr Isaac Brounson & Deacon Thomas Clark Chosen Moderators.

Att the Same Meeting In order to the more Effectual and Speedy Setling High wayes the Matter being Moved to the proprietors and the Matter fully Discoursed they Did by their vote Agree and Conclude to Impower and by their vote do Impower the Towns Committe Appointed Att A Town Meeting January 13th 1734. to Lay out Needfull Highwayes to Agree with perticular persons where Highwayes Run through their Land. and Say what Recompence they Shall have for Dammage Done them and the Committe A Greeing with the persons Damnified. and Makeing Return to the Registers office their Agreement Shall be Sufficient to the holding the Lands Set out to them for A Recompence.

A true Record of the Act

Attest. John Southmayd Clerk.

Att the Same Meeting It was Voted by the proprietors that they would Chuse A Committe to Look After the proprietors timber In the undivided Land that there be no trespass upon It from out town men or Such as have no propriety In the undivided Land And to prosecute the tresspass According to Law. and for A Committe Ensign John Scovill. Lieu^t. Samuel Hikcox and Doc Dan^{ll} Porter Made Choise off.

A true Record of the vote

Attes. Jno. Southmayd Clerk.

Att the Same Meeting with Respect to the North East Corner of the Bounds the proprietors thought It needfull to Appoint A Committe to Make Search wheither our bounds are Stated by the County Survayer and on Record and to Defend our Bounds Att the North East Corner on the North End.

If the proprietors of Hartford and Winsdor west Lands Contest with us.

A true Record of ye Vote

Attes. Jno. Southmayd Clerk.

And for A Committe the proprietors made Choise of Capt. Ephraim Worner Capt William Judd. and Lieu^t. Samuel Hikcox.

A true Record of ye Committe

Att. John Southmayd Clerk.

Att the Same Meeting Deacon Thomas Clark was aded to the Committe Made Choise of November. 26. 1723. to Consider andInspect Certain Difficulties about Some Former Grants.

A true Record of the vote

Attest John Southmayd Clerk.

the Meeting by Vote Adjourned to the Second Tuseday In November Next. 1726. (1736.)

A Copy of the Warrant for the Above S^d Meeting these are there fore In his majesties name to require the proprietors In the Common and undivided Land of S^d Township. of Waterbury to Meet att the publick meeting house In S^d Waterbury on the thirtieth day of this Instant march at Eight of the Clock before noon then and there to Consider the Above S^d Buisness and Other matters that Shall then be Laid before the S^d proprietors here of fail not.

Signed *p* Thomas Jidd Justice peace.

Waterbury March 3^d. 1736.

Atrue Record Attes. Jn°. Southmayd Clerk.

At A meeting of the proprietors In Waterbury Met by Legal Worning on January third. 1738/9 Cap William Judd Chosen Moderator.

the Meeting AdJourned for three Quarters of an Hour and to Meet At Capt. Hopkins.

Met According to AdJournment according to AdJournment.

and Att the Same meeting It was by vote Agreed that we would go upon A division In the Sequester.

A true Record of the vote.

Attest. Jn°. Southmayd proprietors Clerk.

Att the Same meeting It was by Vote Agreed that the Division In the Sequester Shall be and Is here by Concluded to be A Quarter of an Acre on the pound According to Each mans propriety as Entred on Record

Atrue Record of the Vote.

Attes. Jn°. Southmayd Proprietors Clerk.

Att the Same Meeting Haveing Agreed upon A Division In the Sequester It was also voated to Go upon A Division In the undivided Land.

A true Record of the Vote

Attest. John Southmayd proprietors Clerk.

Att the Same meeting It was Agreed upon by vote that the Division In the undivided Land Shall be half an Acre on the pound to Each proprietor According to his propriety as above.

A true Record of the Vote

Attest. Jn°. Southmayd Proprietors Clerk.

Att the Same meeting haveing Agreed upon A Division of Land upon the present proprietors as Entred In our Records or their Assigns It was Agreed upon by Vote to proceed In the following Manner or method that Is to Say that one Lott Shall Determin both the Divisions now Granted of the Quarter Acre In the Sequester and the Half Acre In the undivided Land upon the proprietors as Entered In our Records or their Assigns to be Laid out In the following Method. that Is to Say that one Lott Shall Determin the Divisions now to be Laid out and Granted of the Quarter Acre and half Acre In the Sequester and undivided. As follows. he that Draws the first Lot Shall take up his first Lott In the Sequester and the Last In the undivided Land and he that Draws the Last Lot Shall take his Division In the Sequester. Last and first In the undivided Land and he that Draws the Second Lot Shall take his Division On the Second day In the Sequester. and his Division In the undivided on the Last day but one and So through the whole Lott and According to this order the Divisions now Granted Shall be Regulated and Laid out and In Each of these Divisions the Several proprietors Shall have but one

peice Laid out In the Sequester. and one peice In the undivided Land unless they Can Joyn them to Some of their former Layings out. and then they may have Liberty to Lay out In More peices then one, voated
Atrue Record of the Vote
Attest John Southmayd Proprietors Clark.
Att the Same Meeting It was Agreed on by voat. that the time to begin to Lay out the Division Now Agreed upon Shall begin In the Sequester on the first Day of May Next Ensueing this Meeting and he that draws the first Lott may Lay out his part on the first of Said May and he that Draws the Second Lott. may Lay out his part on the Second of Said may and So Successively through out the Month of may and then to begin Again on the first of September Next in the Afore Said Order till the Sequestred Division Is finished and then to proceed on the Division In the undivided Land In the Same order according to the method of Laying out the Division as All ready Agreed upon In this Meeting.   Voted
Atrue Record of the vote
Attest. John Southmayd proprietors Clerk.
Att the Same Meeting Voted that we will now proceed to A Lot to Regulate the Division Now Agreed upon.
Attest. John Southmayd Pro. Clerk.
At the Same Meeting voted that Mr Samll Hall Draw the Lotts.
Att the Same Meeting Voted that the Lott Now Drawn be put on Record.
Ats. Jno. Southmayd Clerk.
Att the Same Meeting Timothy Porter was Chosen A Committe Man to be with Mr Jos Lewis and Mr James Porter In Lay ing out high wayes In the South west Quarter of the Bounds.
Attest John Southmayd Pro. Clerk.

the meeting by Vot AdJourned to the Last Tuseday
In Aprill Next.

Attest. John Southmayd Proprietors Clerk.

A List of the Order of the Lott Drawn for January 3
1738/9 to be taken up In the Sequester and undivided
Land. Voted to be put on Record.

1	Benjamin Worner Se^r.	40
2	Ebenezer Hikcox	40
3	John Richards Se^r.	144
4	Isaac Brounson Se^r.	180
5	Thomas Barns	40
6	Thomas Richason Ju^r.	40
7	George Welton	40
8	Thomas Worner	180
9	the fourth Pro. Lot will Scot Worner	40
10	Timothy Hopkins	40
11	Ephraim Worner	40
12	Abraham Anddruss Ju^r.	40
13	Joseph Hikcox Se^r.	108
14	Stephen Hopkins	40
15	John Welton Ju^r.	40
16	William Judd	40
17	Ebenezar Richason	40
18	Obadiah Richards Ju^r.	40
19	John Worner Se^r.	162
20	John Richason	40
21	Capt Thomas Judd Williams.	180
22	Joseph Brounson	40
23	Israel Richason	40
24	Lieu Timothy Stanlys. B.	40
25	Thomas Welton	40
26	Thomas Clark	40

27	Daniel Porter Se[r].	171
28	Jeremiah Peck	270
29	Nathaniel Richason	40
30	John Southmayd	270
31	Stephen Welton	40
32	John Judd Ju[r]	40
33	John Worner Se[r] B Lott	40
34	Jonathan Scott Ju[r].	40
35	Thomas Newels	162
36	William Hikcox	40
37	Daniel Porter Ju[r].	40
38	John Scovill Se[r].	144
39	Ebenezar Brounson	40
40	the 150[lb] propriety	150
41	John Welton Se[r].	144
42	John Hikcox Ju[r].	40
43	Thomas Upson	40
44	Edmund Scott Se[r].	180
45	Thomas Richards Se[r].	40
46	Stephen Upson Se[r].	90
47	Benjamin Worner Ju[r]	40
48	Samuel Scott	40
49	Obadiah Scott	40
50	George Scott Ju[r].	40
51	Stephen Upson Ju[r].	40
52	Samuel Standly	40
53	John Carington	108
54	Samuel Worner of Tho	40
55	Richard Porters	90
56	Third proprietor Lot	40
57	Thomas Handcox	180
58	Thomas Anddruss	40
59	Cap[t] Thomas Judd Jones	180
60	John Judd Se[r].	180

61	Daniel Worner	108
62	Benjamin Barns Ju^r.	40
63	Joseph Gailord Ju^r.	40
64	John Newel	180
65	Joseph Gailord Se^r.	144
66	Benjamin Richards	40
67	Joseph Lewis	40
68	the fifth Proprietors Lott	40
69	Sam^{ll} Hikcox Se^r.	180
70	Isaac Brounson Ju^r.	40
71	John Richard Ju^r.	40
72	Samuel Porter	40
73	Thomas Richason Se^r.	90
74	Thomas Brounson	40
75	David Scott	40
76	Timothy Standly Original	180
77	John Gaylord	40
78	John Brounson of Isaac	40
79	Edmund Scott Ju^r.	126
80	John Barns	40
81	Abraham Anddruss Se^r.	144
82	Thomas Hikcox	40
83	John Standly Se^r.	180
84	Obadiah Richards Se^r.	144
85	first Propr Lott	40
86	Phillip Judd	144
87	Robert Scott	40
88	Jonathan Scott Se^r.	90
89	Joseph Hikcox Ju^r.	40
90	Second propri Lott	40
91	School Lott	270
92	John Brounson Se^r.	144
93	Ben Barns Se^r.	180
94	Richard Welton	40

95	George Scott Se⁰.	40
96	Lieu John Hopkins	180
97	John Scovill Ju⁰.	40
98	Thomas Judd Ju⁰.	180
99	The Sixth Pro. Lott	40
100	Abraham Andruss Cooper	180

A true List of the Lott Drawn January 3ᵈ 1738/9.

Attest John Southmayd
Proprietors Clark

At A meeting of the proprietors In Waterbury Met by AdJournment Aprill. 23ᵈ. 1738. at three of the Clock In the After Noon. . . .

Cap William Judd Moderator.

Att the Same Meeting upon the Application of Doctor Ephraim Worner to the proprietors with respect to A .ten Acre Grant Granted by the proprietors and Laid out by A Committe and Since Entred upon and Recovered In the Law by Serg⁰. Richard Welton and Now Held by him his request Is that the proprietors would Grant him Liberty to take up Said ten Acres In Any of the undivided Land not preJudiceing high ways nor former Grants the proprietors by their vote Granted him the Sᵈ Liberty of taking his ten Acres According to His Request but not In Any of the Sequester Land. the Land taken by William Scovill he takeing A Copy of the Act.[1]

att the Same Meeting John Southmayd Ju⁰. was Chosen to Lay out Land In the Sequester.

the meeting AdJourned to the monday before the Election Next

At Ameeting of the proprietors of Waterbury Met

---

[1] This, added later by Thomas Clark.

by AdJournment May 7ᵗʰ 1739. Capᵗ William Judd Moderator.

upon the Memorial of the Society of West bury. And A Citation upon the proprietors of Waterbury to Appear be fore the General Assembly this Instant may the proprietors by their Vote Made Choise of Cap Tim. Hopkins and Capᵗ. Wil. Judd to Represent them

Att the Same Meeting Declared they would not Make Any Alteration about the Draught of the Lott Last drawn for In Giving Any proprietor. the Liberty of more than one Spot to Lay his Land Except what he Joyns to his own Land.

the Meeting AdJourned to the third Tuse day In September Next.

upon the Application of Mʳ J. Smith[1] with Respect to the Seting of his House upon the parsonage Land and A Committe to Adjust that Matter they Concluded to send A Committe upon his Charge they Concurred And Appointed A Committe Cap. Will. Judd. Ensign Thoˢ. Richards. and William Scovill. to Go and View and Make Return to the Town. this Removed to the Town Book.

At Ameeting of the proprietors of Waterbury Met by Ad Journment September 18ᵗʰ. 1739. and no buisness presenting the meeting Ad Journed to the Second monday In December Next Ensueing. . . .

Ameeting of the proprietors of Waterbury Met by adJournment Decem. 10ᵗʰ. 1739. and no buisness

----

[1] The words " the Application " and " Smith " for some reason were crossed out.

presenting the Meeting AdJourned to the 24ᵗʰ of this Instant December.

Att A proprietors Meeting In Waterbury Met According to AdJournment December 24ᵗʰ. 1739. at the Same meeting It was Asked the proprietors Wheither they would do Any thing further with Relation to the Devision Granted January 3ᵈ 1738/9 Answered In the Negative.

Att the Same Meeting It was voated that the Committee for Laying out high wayes In the North East Corner of the bounds Shall have full power to Widen the high way where west bury Meeting house Is Appointed to Stand So as to Accomidate Said House with A Sutable Green according to their Descretion and to Award Satisfaction to the owners of the Land that Said high way Shall take from

A true Record

Attest John Southmayd   Clerk.

the meeting AdJourned to the first monday of Aprill next at twelve A Clock In the Morning.

the first monday of Aprill. 1740. the Moderator and Clerk met according to Ad Jurnment, and no buissness appearing the Meeting ad Journed to the 3ᵈ tuesday in September. 1740. to Meet at. 10 of the Clock.

the Meeting of the proprietors In Waterbury Met according to Ad Journment September 16ᵗʰ 1740. And no buisness the Meeting Ad Journed to the prox day In Aprill. next.

Waterbury Aprill. 13ᵗʰ 1741. the proprietors in Waterbury Met According to AdJournment and No busness

Appearing the Meeting AdJourned to prox day in September Next.

Att A proprietors Meeting In Waterbury January 14th 1745/6 the worning being Given As the Law Directs. by A warrant to the Proprietors and A publick Notification Set up.

M^r. Isaac Brounson Chosen Moderator: at the Same Meeting Some thing Considered About Ameasurer and Concluded not necessary to Chuse one and Some thing Discoursed About John Worner Taylors Bacheldor Lott and Concluded that that buisness ly for A Further Consideration and Also Some thing About the Line between Farmington and us which was Also thought best to be dismist to A meeting In March Next and Accordingly the Meeting adjourned by Vote to the Second Tuseday In March Next at 10 Clock fore noon.

Att A proprietors Meeting In Waterbury Met by AdJournment March 11th 1745/6
the Meeting AdJourned for 3 Quarters of An Hour. and then meet According to AdJurnment
att the Same Meet. about Farmington line.   It was put to Vote wheither they would do Any thing In that Matter.   Voated In the Affirmative.
    Att the Same Meeting It was Agreed by Vote that they will be att the Charge of the Sute In Setling the line between farmington and Waterbury.
    Att the Same Meeting Ebenezer Worner 3^d and George Nichols put In their Petition with Respect to John Worners Tailors bacheldor Lot which was Said to be forfited and they had bought and petitioned for the Several devisions Laid out upon A bacheldor Lott. In the Words following: To the worshipfull moderator

ii

and Gentlemen Proprietors of the Town of Waterbury
at their proprietors Meeting Held In S^d Waterbury
the Eleventh day of March 1745/6 the Petition of
George Nichols and Ebenezer Worner the third Humbly Sheweth that where as the Town of Waterbury at
their Meeting held by the proprietors of S^d Town on the
23^d day of December. 1701. Accepted John Worner
Tayler an Inhabitant and proprietor on A bacheldors
Right upon which admition the Said Worner was to
Have and was Entitled to thirty Eight Acres of Land
meadow and Includeing Ahome Lott. and four Acres
of pasture In Fee on Condition he did Inhabit five
years In the Town and build or purchase A Dwelling
House Sixteen foot Square and It Appearing on Record
that he purchased A Dwelling House and Lott of
Daniel Worner June 25th 1705. and Was An Inhabitant
till October the third 1713 where by It Appears he full
filled Said Conditions of Settlement and thereby became Intitled to All the Divisions of Land In Said
Waterbury Equal to those Accepted as And Called by
the name of Bacheldors to which was Granted to Each
at their Settlement thirty Eight Acres of Land In
Said Town of Waterbury Soon After an addition of 30
Acres More and In February 28 1701/2 was Granted to
Each Bacheldor Right 55 Acres of Land. and on 26th
of November 1723 Granted A further Division of 40
Acres and In March 13th 1727 Granted A further divi-
sion of forty Acres More and on the third of January
1738/9 Granted A Division of twenty Acres and also A
Division of ten Acres In the Sequestred Lands and
Soon After Sixteen Acres and 20 Rods In the Village
In the Whole Amounting to 249 acres and 20 Rods of
Land which Divisions have been All Actually Granted
Survayed and Laid out to and on the Said Bacheldors

Rights Exclusive of and Omiting the Said John Worner who hath not had Any part Share or Division In S^d Town but has been Wholly Omited. and your petitioners Supposeing S^d Worners title to S^d Several Devisions of Land to be Good and Vallid purchused the Same of the Said John Worner as may Appear by his Deed Exicuted In due form of Law. to your Petitioners Dated Aprill 22. 1743. and Recorded Where upon your petitioners Humbly pray that.

That the Gentle men proprietors of the Said Town of Waterbury would please to take the Matter in to their Consideration. (not In the Least Doubting that they are freely Willing to Rectify Any part Omisions or Mistakes) And to Grant to their petitioners what In Law and Justice to the S^d Worner Appertains and Grant to their Petitioners In Right of S^d John Worner An Equivelent for those Lands and Devisions Omited. to be taken up In the Common and undivided Lands In S^d Waterbury where It may be found So as Not to Encroach on Highways Sequestred Lands or on Any perticular Survays and that A Committe may be Appointed to Lay out the Same at the proper Charge and Cost of your Petitioners or In Some Other way as you In your Wisdom Shall think best Grant your Petitioners Relief. In the premises and your petitioners Shall as In duty bound &c.

March 11th 1745/6   Ebenezer Worner ye 3^d
                                George Nichols.

After the pleas And Arguing for and Against the petition being heard the Question was put wheither they would do Any thing on the Petition   Voted In the Negative

the Meeting AdJourned to the Last Monday In March Instant.

At A meeting of the proprietors of Waterbury Met According to Ad Journment March 31 An Dom. 1746.

att the Same Meeting with Respect to the Village Lotts So Called It Appearing that the Setling the line between Woodbury and Waterbury Against the Village Lots has Altered the Highwayes there It was by Vote Agreed and Concluded to Appoint a Committee to Lay out the High way In S⁴ Village According to Sequestration and paralel with the Settled line between Woodbury and Waterbury that the proprietors of the Lots there may be under advantages to Remove their bound East or West to bring them Into the line of Said High wayes.

Voted and Atrue Record of the Vote

Test. John Southmayd Proprietors Clark.

Att the Same Meeting Voted that the Committe to Lay out Highwayes In Westbury are Impowered to Lay out the Highways In the Village as Agreed upon In the Above Vote.

atrue Record of vote.

Test. Jnᵒ Southmayd Proᵗʳˢ Clerk.

Att the Same Meeting It Appearing that the Town Had Appointed A Committe to Act In their behalf In prepareing A Settlement of the line between Farmington and Waterbury the proprietors by Vote Appoint and Impower the Same Committe. to Act In their behalf and represent them In S⁴ Affair if Need be

Atrue Record of of the Vote

Test. Jnᵒ Southmayd Proprietors Clerk.

Att the Same Meeting. Ensign Daniel Southmayd was appointed and Impowered to Lay out Highwayes

In the North East Quarter with Lieuᵗ. John Scovill and Lieuᵗ. John Judd

A true Record

Test. Jnº. Southmayd Pro: Clerk.

Att the Same Meeting It was Voted that they would Sell proprietors undivided Land to pay the Above Charges.

A true Record

Test. Jnº. Southmayd Pro: Clerk.

att the Same Meeting voted that there Should be 100 Acres of Land Sold to Defray the Proprietors Charge and Anote from the Clark to Lay It out Receiving order from yᵉ Committe Sufficient.

Att the Same Meeting. Lieuᵗ. Jnº. Scovill Capᵗ. Samˡˡ. Hikcox and Capᵗ Willᵐ. Judd were Appointed A Committe to Make Sale of the 100 Acres of Land and Lodge the money with the Proprietors Treasurer taking his Recept for the Same voted

A true Record of the vote

Test Jnº Southmayd Proprietors Clerk.

Att the Same meeting John Southmayd was Chosen Proprietors Treasurer.

Att the Same Meeting It was by Vote Agreed and Concluded that when the Said Committe have Sold A parcel of Land the Committe Shall ord the proprietors Clerk to Give Anote to the person Directed to the Measures to Lay out So much Land to that person which Shall be Sufficient for his haveing and holding of the Land from the proprietors and Every Other person.

A true Record of the Vote

Test John Southmayd Proprietors Clerk.

the Meeting adJourned by Vote to the first Monday of November Next.

At A proprietors Meeting Met According to AdJournment the first monday of November. 1746.

At the Same meeting upon the Motion of Doc^t Daniel Porter about A ten Acre pitch. which his Father bought of Thos Judd of Hartford which he Declar'd Neither S^d Judd nor His father nor His Heirs Ever had Taken up which he Desired to have Liberty to take up. where upon the proprietors Appointed Jno. Southmayd and Lieu^t Jno Scovill to Inspect that Matter and If they find It has not been had yn the Clerk to Grant An order to the Measurer to Lay him out that is to the Doctor 10 Acres In the undivided Land. a note Given for Ten Acres according to this vote.

The Meeting AdJourned by Vote to the Next Monday the 2^d Monday of November.

The Meeting of the proprietors According to AdJournment on the Second Monday In November. 1746. and the Meeting Declared to be Opened.

at the Same Meeting the proprietors appointed Auditors to Audit the Accompts with the Proprietors Treasurer of the Money Commited to him that the Hundred Acres was Sold for and the Committe Appointed were D. Thomas Clark Capt Stephen Upson Capt Thomas Hikcox.

Att the Same Meeting: the proprietors. appointed the Above named Committe to tax the Commtes bills that were Improved. In Setling the bounds between Farmington and Waterbury.

At the Same Meeting the proprietors by A vote A Gree to Carry the case between Farmington and Waterbury In to the Common Law.

A true vote of the proprietors.

Test Jno Southmayd Clerk.

Att the Same Meeting. they by their Vote Agreed that the Committe Formerly Appointed to Sell the 100 Acres of Land to Carry on the Sute between Farmington and Waterbury Shall have Liberty to Make Sale of one Hundred Acres more of the proprietors Land for the Above S^d purpose the Meeting AdJourned by vote to the first tuse day after the Second Monday In December Next. At Nine Clock In morning.

On December 9th. 1746 the Proprietors In Waterbury Met According to Ad Journment And Nothing Done and the Meeting adJourned by Vote to the Last Monday In March Next.

At A proprietors Meeting In Waterbury Met According to AdJournment March 30th. 1747 the Meeting Opened. at the Same Meeting the Question was Asked wheither they would remeasure the Village Lotts Answered In the Negative.

Att the Same Meeting the proprietors by vote Agree and Declare that None of the Measurers In the Several Quarters of the Town bounds Shall have Any power to Go Into the Village and lay out Any of the Lots there with out A Perticular and A Special order from the proprietors and what has been done there of that Nature Shall be Counted In Vallid and is here by Made voide. Voted

A true Record Test. John Southmayd Clerk.

Att the Same Meeting the proprietors by Vote Agree. to Appointed A Committe to Go in to the Village So Called and bring the bounds of the Several Lotts there Into the line of the highways as Laid out by Alate Committe with the help of Capt Knowls of Woodbury the Same Weadth as the Lots were Laid by the Com-

mitte appointed to Lay out the Village Lots and Make
Return of the Certain boundaries and Weadth of Each
Lott. Voted
Atrue Record of the Vote.

Test John Southmayd Clerk.

the Meeting of March 30ᵗʰ 1747 Continued
Att the Same meeting for A Committe were Appoin-
ted Capᵗ Timothy Hopkins. George Welton and Sergᵗ
Thomas Porter by Vote.

Atrue Record Test Jnº Southmayd Clerk.

Att the Same Meeting It was by Vote Agreed and
Concluded that the Committe to Lay out Highwayes
In the Several Quarters of the Town Shall have no
Farther Power to Give proprietors Land for Dam-
mage done by Highways running through perticular
mens Land and do here by put A stop to It till the
Proprietors Shall order Other Wise. voted
Atrue Record of the Vote

Test. Jnº Southmayd Clerk.

Att the Same Meeting the Meeting adJourned by
Vote to the first Tuseday in November Next.

Meet Acording to AdJournment the first Tuseday
In November 1747 And but few of the proprietors
Met and the Meeting adJourned to the Second Tuse-
day In January Next.

January the twelfth 1747/8 the proprietors Met
According to AdJournment.
At the Same Meeting after Some Considerable
Discourse About A Division In the undivided Land
Voted that they would Have A Division In the un-
divided Land.

At the Same It was Agreed and Voted that they would have a division of one Quarter of an Acre on the pound In the undivided Land.

At the Same meeting It was Agreed and voated that A Lott drawn upon the Several Proprietors Shall regulate the Above sd Division.

At the Same meeting It was by vote Agreed that the order of the division Should be in the Following Manner and form that Is to Say. he that has the first Lot Shall have the first turn to Lay out his Land and the Second the Second and the third the third Turn and So Successively till they have all taken up their Lands as here After Shall be Agreed upon.

At the Same Meeting It was by Vote Agreed that the first Lott Drawn Shall Lay out his Lott on the Sixteenth day of Aprill Next If Apropper day for the Work and the 2^d on the Next proper day and So Successively till the Last day of may next. and then to begin Again on the first day of September following if A proper day and So to Go on In the Same order Succesively till the Lot be finished.   Excepting Saboths and all publick dayes and Such dayes when the Weather Is unsutable In the Judge ment of the Measurers applied to and he whose turn falls on one of the Excepted days Shall Improve the Next proper Day to take up his Land and he that neglects to take up his Lott on his proper day as above limited Shall loose his turn So as not to hinder any other man of his proper day.

At the Same Meeting It was Voted and Agreed that Every man In Laying out his Lott In his turne to Accommodate him Self. Shall have Liberty to Lay It in Severall peices by his own Land handsomely formed. and where men Dont lay It by their own Land they Shall Lay It in one peice and In A hand Some form provided there be Land Enough In the place.

Att the Same Meeting the proprietors finding A Sequestration made At west bury of three Mile Square In the Center of Said Society Made At A meeting of the proprietors March 13. 1733. the proprietors by their Vote take of the Sequestration and It is here by Set A—side and made Voide

Att the Same Meeting the proprietors made Choise of Cap' William Judd A Committe man to be Aded to their former Committe to Mannage In the Affair Aganst Farmington

the Meeting AdJourned to the first Tuse day In February Next to Eight of the Clock in the Morning In order to Draw A Lott on the Division Now Agreed upon.

At the Above meeting January 12ᵗʰ 1747/8 upon the Request of Deaⁿ Jnᵒ Worner of North bury that he might have Liberty to relinquish Apeice of Land that he had taken up adjoyning to his own Land and Laping upon Some Other Lands and Lay It in Another place the proprietors by their Vote Gave him the Liberty he desired provided he would Give A Quit Claim of the Above Said Land unto the proprietors and be at all the Charges and then the Clark to Give A note to the Measurer to Lay It out In Another place.

Att A meeting of the proprietors Met by Ad Journment Febʸ. 2ᵈ 1747/8.

At the Same Meeting In order to the Drawing of the Lott Agreed upon the Last meeting. Mʳ. Levenworth Introducing the Matter by prayer by Avote of the proprietors Mʳ. Levenworth was Appointed to Draw the Lott.

At the Same Meeting the Lott was Drawn according to the Vote of of the proprietors Above. and Entred as on the Other Side this Leaf.

Attest Jn° Southmayd Proprietors Clark.

Att the Same Meeting It was by Vote Agreed that the Committe prosecute the buisness between Farmington and us at the Next Superior Court.

Att the Same Meeting It was by Vote Agreed that the Committe Sell Another Hundred Acres of the proprietors Land for the Carriing on of the buisness.

. The Meeting AdJourned by Vote to the Second Tuseday In Aprill Next.—

We the Subscribers being Neighbours to m^r Ebenezer Bradly of North bury Do Certify that we Esteem him ye Said Bradly an Honest Industrous man and that he and his family are Likely to prove wholesom Inhabitants Waterbury February 26. 1759

Ebenezer Ford	Thomas Blakslee
Asahel Castel	Jacob Blakslee
Isaac Castel	Gideon Allin
John How	Moses Blakslee
Ebenezer Curtice	Ebenezer Allin[1]

The order of the Lott Drawn on the Division Granted In the undivided Land Granted January 12th 1747/8. Drawn February 2^d 1747/8.

1	Robert Scott	40
2	David Scott	40
3	Ebenezer Brounson	40
4	Timothy Hopkins	40
5	Thomas Richard Se^r	40
6	Samuel Stanly	40

[1] Ebenezer Bradley had been warned to leave the town.

7	4th Proprietors Lott. S. W.	40
8	John Hopkins	180
9	150^{lb} propriety	150
10	John Barns	40
11	John Hikcox	40
12	Thomas Upson	40
13	Ebenezer Richason	40
14	John Scovill Se^r	144
15	2^d Proprietors Lott	40
16	Thomas Clark	40
17	Daniel Porter Ju^r	40
18	Ephraim Worner.	40
19	Thomas Anddruss	40
20	John Richason	40
21	6th Proprietors Lott	40
22	Thomas Judd Jones	180
23	Richard Porter	90
24	John Richards Se^r	144
25	Stephen Hopkins	40
26	Joseph Gailard Ju^r	40
27	John Judd Se^r	180
28	John Brounson Se^r	144
29	George Scott Se^r	40
30	first Proprietors Lott	40
31	Thomas Brounson	40
32	Abraham Anddruss Ju^r	40
33	Benjamin Barns Ju^r	40
34	John Carrington	108
35	Joseph Gaylord Se^r	144
36	Thomas Hikcox	40
37	Daniel Worner	108
38	Jno Worner. Se^r Bach	40
39	John Gaylord	40
40	Thomas Richason Se^r	90

41	John Scovill Ju'	40
42	Jonathan Scott Ju'	40
43	William Judd	40
44	John Welton Ju'	40
45	Stephen Upson Se'	90
46	Isaac Brounson Ju'	40
47	Israel Richason	40
48	Abraham Anddruss Cooper	180
49	Benjamin Worner Se'	40
50	Thomas Barns	40
51	Benjamin Barns Se'	180
52	Jonathan Scott Se'	90
53	the 5ᵗʰ Proprietors Lott	40
54	Thomas Judd William	180
55	Timothy Stanly Original	180
56	Thomas Richason Ju'	40
57	Isaac Brounson Se'	180
58	Benjamin Richards	40
59	John Welton Se'	144
60	Obadiah Scott	40
61	Timothy Stanly Bachel	40
62	John Worner Se'	162
63	Thomas Newel	162
64	William Hikcox	40
65	Jeremiah Peck	270
66	Stephen Welton	40
67	Thomas Judd Ju' Halls	180
68	Samuel Scott	40
69	Stephen Upson Ju'	40
70	George Scott Ju'	40
71	Samuel Porter	40
72	John Brounson of Isaac	40
73	Obadiah Richards Ju'	40
74	Daniel Porter Se'	171

75	Thomas Worner Se[r]	180
76	Obadiah Richard Se[r]	144
77	Sam[ll] Hikcox Se[r]	180
78	Samuel Worner of Tho[s]	40
79	John Richards Ju[r]	40
80	George Welton	40
81	John Judd Ju[r]	40
82	Abraham Anddruss Se[r]	144
83	Nathaniel Richason	40
84	Joseph Brounson	40
85	Edmund Scott Ju[r]	126
86	Benj. Worner Ju[r]	40
87	Edmund Scott Se[r]	180
88	Richard Welton	40
89	Thomas Handcox	180
90	Phillip Judd	144
91	Thomas Welton	40
92	Joseph Hickcox Se[r]	108
93	Joseph Lewis	40
94	John Newe	180
95	John Southmayd	270
96	School Lott	270
97	John Stanly Se[r]	180
98	Joseph Hickcox Ju	40
99	Ebenezer Hickcox'	40
100	the 3[d] Proprietors Lott	40

A true List of the Lott Drawn February 2[d] 1747/8.

Test. Jn[o] Southmayd Clerk.

The proprietors Met According to y[e] Ad Journment the Second Tuseday of Aprill Anno Dom. 1748. and the Meeting Opened.

At the Same meeting the proprietors by Vote Agreed that the proprietors would be at the Charge of paying the fine. for Not perambulateing with Farmington if they Should Site the Town to per Ambulate this Spring and Should Exact the fine.

Att the Same Meeting. to Explain an Act of the proprietors for not paying for Any More Highways Voted that the Act Extended only to highways that Should be lay'd out After the Act and Not to Any former highways the Meeting adJourned by Vote to the first Tuseday In October Next.

At A meeting of the Proprietors. In Waterbury Met December. 23^d. 1751 being Worned According to Law. by A notification Set on the Sign post and Worrant Directed to James Nichols for the Worning of the Same the Notification and Warrant Dated November 23^d. 1751.

Signed by John Southmayd Justice of peace.

Daniel Southmayd Chosen Moderator. and then proceeded to the buisness and first Considered About High ways. wheither they would pay for Any more High ways or Not. as yet. Voted In the Negative.

at the Same Meeting It was Voted that the proprietors Committe for the Laying out of Highway. Dissist from that buisness for the present and till Farther order from the proprietors at A regular meeting of the proprietors.

at the Same Meeting the proprietors Entred upon discourse about A Division In the undivided land and It was Voted to have A Division In the Common and undivided Land.

Att the Same Meeting It was voted that the Division now Agreed Shall be Half An Acre on the pound to Each proprietor.

At the Same Meeting It was Voted that In the

Division Now Agreed upon there Shall Shall be two Lotts and one Draught to Decide the Lotts. he that Draws the first Lott. In the Draught to Lay out his Land on the first Day of Laying Out the first Lott. and the Last day of Laying out the 2ᵈ Lott and he that Draws the Last Lott to have the Last day In the first Lott and the first day In the Second Lott. and So Successively of all the Rest. and John Southmayd to prepare the Lott Against the Next Meeting

Att the Same Meeting It was Agreed by Vote to be Gin to Lay out the Lotts on the 20ᵗʰ of March next.

Att the Same Meeting It was voted and Enacted that the Severall proprietors Committees to Lay out Lands In their Several Quarters Shall have power where they have In Laying out Land Lapt upon Other Mens Land. when It Shall Come to their Certain Knowledge Make up the Lapt Land In Another place to him whose Land falls Short.   the meeting adjourned by vote to the first Monday In February next.

the order of the Lott drawn on the Division Granted December 23ᵈ 1751 of half an Acre on the pound In the undivided Land

1	Joseph Lewis	40
2	3ᵈ proprietors Lott	40
3	Thomas Clark	40
4	Thomas Worner Seʳ	180
5	John Scovill Juʳ	40
6	Samuell Scott	40
7	Benjamin Worner Juʳ	40
8	Isaac Brounson Juʳ	40
9	John Hopkins	180
10	John Stanly Seʳ	180
11	Stephen Upson Juʳ	40

12	Israel Richason	40
13	John Scovill Se^r	144
14	Samuell Hickcox Se^r	180
15	Joseph Hickcox Ju^r	40
16	Isaac Brounson Se^r	180
17	Thomas Judd Ju^r	180
18	Jonathan Scott Se^r	90
19	Richard Welton	40
20	Thomas Richason Se^r	90
21	John Worner Se^r B.	40
22	Timothy Stanly Original	180
23	Edmund Scott Ju^r	126
24	Thomas Newel	162
25	Benjamin Worner	40
26	Nathaniel Richason	40
27	John Gailord	40
28	Samuel Porter	40
29	Stephen Upson Se^r	90
30	John Carrington	108
31	Timothy Stanly B. L.	40
32	Abraham Anddruss Co	180
33	Joseph Brounson	40
34	Obadiah Scott	40
35	William Judd B. L.	40
36	Edmund Scott Se^r	180
37	Samuel Worner Tho:	40
38	Robert Scott	40
39	Joseph Gailord Ju^r	40
40	John Richards Ju^r	40
41	John Brounson Se^r	144
42	Thomas Brounson	40
43	Benjamin Barns Se^r	180
44	Ebenezer Hickcox	40
45	Daniel Porter Ju^r	40

12

46	4th Proprietors Lott	40
47	Abraham Anddruss Se^r	144
48	John Judd Ju^r	40
49	School Lott	270
50	5th Proprietors Lott	40
51	Thomas Anddrus	40
52	John Judd Se^r	180
53	Ebenezer Richason	40
54	Jonathan Scott Ju^r	40
55	John Richard Se^r	144
56	John Barns	40
57	Timothy Hopkins	40
58	Thomas Welton	40
59	John Welton Se^r	144
60	Thomas Handcox	40
61	Benjamin Richard	40
62	John Welton Ju^r	40
63	George Scott Se^r	40
64	Richard Porter	90
65	2^d proprietors Lott	40
66	John Southmayd	270
67	George Welton	40
68	David Scott	
69	Ebenezer brounson	40
70	Stephen Welton	40
71	150 ^{ll} propriety	150
72	Obadiah Richards Se^r	144
73	Phillip Judd	144
74	Thomas Judd William	180
75	John Worner Se^r	162
76	6th proprietors Lott	40
77	Thomas Richards	40
78	Jeremiah Peck	270
79	Joseph Gaylord Se^r	144

80	Ephraim Worner	40
81	first proprietors Lott	40
82	Thomas Judd Jones	180
83	Benjamin Barn Ju'	40
84	Stephen Hopkins	40
85	John Hickcox	40
86	Thomas Richason Ju'	40
87	William Hickcox	40
88	Thomas Hickcox	40
89	Abraham Anddruss Ju'	40
90	Daniel Porter Se'	171
91	John Newel	180
92	Samuel Stanly	40
93	George Scott Ju'	40
94	Thomas Upson	40
95	Daniel Worner	108
96	John Brounson of Isaac	40
97	John Richason	40
98	Thomas Barns	40
99	Joseph Hickcox Se'	108
100	Obadiah Richard Ju'	40

the Meeting Met According to Ad Journment the first Monday In February 1751 and Met according to AdJournment the MoDerator Appointed to Draw the Lott.

At the Same Meeting Lieu' John Scovill A Committe man to be with the Committe formerly Made viz. George Welton and Lieu' Thomas Porter to Cary out the boundaries of the Several Lots In the Village to the Several Highway as the proprietors of the Lots Shall Call them. and to Make Returns of their Certain bounds So that they May be Entred on Record and ascertained on Record.

att the Same Meeting Ebenezer Worner of Daniel laying before this Meeting that Apiece of Land formerly Laid out to him of of two Acres and A Quarter between the great Hill and Strait mountains Entred In Waterbury Record 2^{d} book page 725 was Spoiled by two High wayes being Laid through It. and Desireing Liberty to take It in some Other place. It was voted that upon his Giving A Quit Claim to the proprietors of Said peice. he might have Liberty to take up four Acres and half In Some Other place In the undivided Land provided he would be at the Cost of It.

att the Same Meeting upon the Motion of Stephen Judd In behalf of Doctor Ebenezer Worner of Woodbury Desiring that he might Lay out Eleven Acres and Quarter of Land In the undivided Land In Said Waterbury In Lew of Eleven Acres and Quarter of boggy meadow In A meadow west of Break Neck Hill that he had Liberty to take as his part of A division Granted on his Fathers propriety the Land In Sd Meadow being taken up Voted that he might take So much In any of the undivided Land provided he gave A Quit Claim to the proprietors of All his Right In Said Meadow by Vertue of Said Grant and be Att the Cost there of

the Meeting AdJourned to 2^{d} Monday In March.

Att A meeting of the proprietors. In Waterbury March 9th 1752 According to AdJournment

Att the Same Meeting. upon the Motion of the Heirs of Daniel Porter deceased wheither they would Consider them upon the Account of Some dispositions of Land formerly Made by the proprietors. which was protested against by their Father when the Same was Acted. Voted In the Negative

Att the Same Meeting upon the Request and Motion of Lieu' Thomas Richards. with Respect to Some Village Lotts. which he Suppose to Want Measure. after Considerable Discourse upon the Matter the proprietors by Vote Impowered the former Committe upon the Motion and Att the Charge of the Said Richards to Go up on the Spot. and remeasure the Land with In Said Richards Bounds. and if there be not So much Land as to answer the village Lotts and his Other Lands then they Shall make It up to him In the undivided Land and to do the Same by Any of the Village Lotts upon the owners request and Charge.   Voted.

Att the Same Meeting the proprietors Voted that they will desist from laying Laying out the Last Granted Division on the first of June Next and begin Again on the first of September and then Go on with the Said Division Regulateing all Other affairs according to our Method In Laying out the Division In 1723.

At the Same Meeting upon the Motion of Doc' Thomas foot that he Wanted About 13 Acres and Some Rods of Land In his Village Lotts. the proprietors Granted him the high way at the west End of of his Village Lotts the weadth of his Lots as A Recompence for Said Land wanting and he Acepted of the Same and Declared him Self Satisfied.

the Meeting AdJourned to the first monDay of September Next.   At nine of the Clock In the fore Noon.

The proprietors Met according to the AdJurnment 2ᵈ Monday of September 1752. a few proprietors Met and No buisness Appearing the Meeting AdJourned to the first Monday In March Next at nine of the clock in the fore noon the proprietors Met According to AdJournment March 5th 1753.

Att the Same Meeting upon the Motion of the Town Committe It was Voted that the proprietors Shall Allow Somany Acres of Land to be taken up In the undivided Land of the Town as there Are Acres of Land taken for y^e. Necessary High way out of the Survays of perticular persons and A Committe Appointed by the Town And proprietors to Lay out to Exchange And Alter High wayes Shall have full power and Authority to Exchange or Other wise to Dispose of the undivided Lands as Is Above Mentioned In this Act. for the purpose Afore Said.

And Itis Also Voted that All Necessary High ways that Shall be Laid out through the Undivided Land by the Committe Appointed by the Town and proprietors for that purpose Shall be free for the Towns use provided they are Not Wider than four Rods.

at the Same Meeting It was Also Voted that the Committe Appointed for Laying out High wayes In the Several Quarters of the Town Shall have power to Exchange Such high wayes as Now are or here After Shall Appear to be unnecessary for Such High ways as Are Needfull or other wayes dis pose of Such unnecessary high way as the Committe In Whose Quarter they are Shall find Most advantagious for the purchaseing those that Are Necessary And Such unnecessary Highway Shall Enure to the benifit of the proprietors. this meeting AdJourned by Vote to the first Monday In Aprill next to Meet at nine A Clock In the Morning at the Meeting house.

the proprietors Met on the first Mondy of Aprill 1753.
the Proprietors Made Choise of Capt William Judd
Moderator

At the Same Meeting After Some discourse About
In Croachments upon upon the proprietors Land. It was
Concluded and voted to Make Choise of two men to be
Joyned with the Survayor In Each Quarter as A
Committe to take Care that the proprietors Land be
not In Croached upon and they Made Choise of Capt
Daniel Southmayd and Lieu^t Tomas Porter with Dea
Thomas Clark and M^r. Joseph Brounson and Serg
Ebenezer Richards with Cap William Judd and Serg^t
John Lewis and Mr Isaac Brounson with M^r. James
Porter and M^r. James Nichols and Lieu^t. John Scovill
with Lieu^t. John Judd.

Att the Same Meeting upon the motion of the Heirs
of Abraham Anddruss Cooper or Ju^r with Respect
to Severall Antient Grants found upon Record belonging to their father limiting them to A Certain Spot
which was Supposed to be taken up by Other men and
their father nor they not to have had their Land. It
was Voted and In Acted that if the Said Heirs would
Give A Quit Claim to the proprietors of All their Right
and Claim to those former Grants and pitches So that
they Should or Could not have Any further demands
or Claims upon the proprietors with Respect there to.
and be at All the Charges then the Said Heirs might
have Liberty to take up Eighteen Acres In Any of the
undivided Lands In Said Town ship of Waterbury
Except the Sequester.

an order to Jonathan prindle for Said Land 18
Acres[1]

---

[1] Added at a later date.

the Meeting adJourned to the first monday In
November Next.

Waterbury In New Haven County the proprietors
met According to AdJurnment on the first Monday
of November 1753 and but A few proprietors and No
buisness Appearing the Meeting was by Vote adJourned
to the first Munday of february next At Nine of the
Clock In fore Noon.

February 4th 1754 the proprietors Met According
to AdJournment.

At the Same Meeting upon the Discourse about the
high way that was Laid out between Obadiah Richards
and Richardes Eight Acre Lott So Called to the
pasage through Isaacs meadow It was Voted that the
Select Men that Laid out said High way Shall have
full power to Agree With the person through whose
Land Its Laid provided there be Sufficient Land at
Said place to do It.

the Meeting AdJourned to the Last munday In
March Next at Nine of the Clock.

Waterbury March 25th A. D. 1754. the proprietors
of Waterbury Met According to Ad Journment being
the Last monday In Said Month.

At the Same Meeting Phineas Royse was Chosen
A Survayor of Highways In the North East Quarter
to Joyn Lieu^t Scovill and Jn° Judd the former Committe.

at the Same Meeting It was voted that they would
appoint A Committe to Search and find out how our
bounds are Setled on the North End.

At the Same Meeting Capt. Sam^{ll} Hickcox was made
Choise of.

att the Same meeting It Was voted they would Sell Some Land for the Expence of Making the Above Said Expences

Att the Same Meeting the Same Meeting It was voted there should be Sold ten Acres of Land Land to the Highest bider and for A Committe to Sel the Land D. Thomas Brounson and James Nichols at the Same Meeting It was Voted that those that bid of the ten Acres Shall have Liberty to take It In the undivided or Sequester as will Suit the buyer.

the Meeting AdJourned to the third Tuseday In Aprill next at one of the Clock Afternoon.

At A meeting of the proprietors In Waterbury Met According to AdJournment Aprill 16th 1754:

at the Same Meeting After A Great deal of Discourse About Our North west Antient bounds Capt Judd and Lieut Jno Scovill were appointed to Make Search and Enquiry About that Antient boundary. to find It out Inorder to the Stateing of Aline between us and Hartford and winsdor proprietors

Att the Same Meeting the proprietors Appointed Mr Thomas Matthews And Capt Samll Hickcox their Agents to Represent them In Any Court and Action that Shall be Commenced Against them.

the Meeting AdJourned by Vote to the Last monday In May Next at one of the Clock.

the proprietors Met According to AdJournment the Last Monday In May 1754.—att the Same Meeting where as there was In A former meeting Agents Appointed to Represent the proprietors In Any Court In Any Action that Shall be Commenced Against them they do now Appoint and Impower the Same Agents to Commence Any Action or Suit Against Any Town or person In behalf of the proprietors that Shall be thought necessary for the benefit. and advantage of the proprietors voted

Att the Same Meeting It was Voted that they would Give Liberty to Sell twenty Acres of Land In the Sequester or undivided Land to be Sold on the 2ᵈ Monday of June Next. at Public vandue to the Highest Bider and the money to be Imployed to pay proprietors Charges and the buyer to have three Months Credit and to Give Small notes for the money and the ten Acres formerly Granted to be Sold to be Sold at the Same time. and under the Same Scircumstances and the Money to be Converted to the Same use.

Att the Same Meeting Lieuᵗ Thomas Brounson and James Nichols appointed Vandue Masters to Sell Said Land

Att the Same It was Voated they would Appoint A Committe to Settle the bounds of the Meadow Lots Laid out by an Antient Committee According to the Intent and Meaning of that Committe So near as Can be Come at and to be done att the request of the owners of the Lotts and at their Charge and for A Committe Deaⁿ Thomas Clark Sergᵗ John Lewis and Sergᵗ Samuel Scott

The meeting adJourned by vote to the first Tuesday of October Next.

The proprietors Met according to AdJournment on the first Tuseday In October A D. 1754. and very few of the proprietors Met and No buisness appearing the Meeting by Vote AdJourned to the first Tuseday after the first Monday In December Next.

Waterbury December 3^d 1754 the proprietors met According to AdJournment and but A few proprietors Appeared and no buisness before them the meeting Was adJourned to the first Tuseday of March Next to meet at Nine of the Clock In the Morning

The proprietors Met According to AdJournment on the first Tuseday of March A. D. 1755
at the Same meeting they made Chose and made Choise of Capt Thomas Porter A Committe man In the Room of James Nichols to Sel proprietors Land and Gather in and pay the money To the Town Treasurer. the meeting AdJourned to the 2^d Tuseday of Aprill Next at nine of the Clock In the fore none up on Consideration of Remeasureing the bounds Granting A new Division and Selling proprietors Land.

The proprietors Met According to AdJournment on the Second Tuseday In Aprill A D. 1755 and no buisness Appearing the Meeting AdJourned to the Last Tuseday In September Next to Meet at ten of the Clock In the fore Noon.

The Proprieters met acording to adJurnment on the Last Tusday of September and few Propriaters and no bisnes apearing the Meating adJurned to the first Tusday of Febuary next to meat at Ten of the Clock in the morning.

The proprietors Met according to Adjornment on the firs Tuesday of February A D 1756   At ye Same meeting Thomas Clark was Chosen proprietors Clerk.
At ye Same meeting Timothy Clark was Chosen measurer for the South East quarter of the bound with his father.

at the Same Meeting Mesu^{rs} Capt Stephen Upson
Thomas Barns Stephen Hopkins ware Chosen A Com-
mitee to adjust accounts with Capt Hikcox Lieu^t John
Scovel Capt Thomas Porter.

At the Same Meeting Mesu^{rs} John Judd Joseph
Bronson & Stephen Upson Junr was Chosen to apprize
the Common Land which Lies within m^r Stephen
Hopkins farm and Make Return to Next meeting.

Voted to AdJorn this Meeting to ye third Tuesday
of Instant February at 9 of ye Clock In ye Morning—

The Meeting met according to adjornment on February 17: 1756

At ye Same meeting voted that if ye Town will by
their vote pay one half of ye Charg that ye proprietors
are at In ye Cause between Harrington and this Town
they will yet Continue their vote as to paying Land for
highways other wise not the Town to have ye benefit
of the bill of Cost if any be obtained.

and for a Commitee to Lay the above vote before ye Town m^r Sam^{ll} Hikcox Thomas porter was
Chosen

the Same meeting voted to Raise Rate of one farthing
on ye pound Lawfull money In Luw of ye half farthing
Granted the Last meeting to be Collected by the first
Day of may next or an Equilent in old tenor in Case y^e
money be paid by that time.

with Respect to ye above Sd Com-tee Chosen to
apprize ye Common Land which Lyes with in m^r
Stephen Hopkins farm have Returned their Doings
to this meeting In ye following manner viz.

viz Waterbury February 17: A D 1756 we the Subscribers being appoynted a Commitee to apprize the
undivided Land at m^r Stephen Hopkins farm Do

Judg it to be worth Six Shillings Lawfull money per
Acre   John Judd
                Joseph Bronson   } Com-tee
                Stephen Upson jur
   At ye Same Meeting Lieu^t John Judd was Chosen
proprietors Treasurer
   at ye Same meeting voted that no measurer Shall
Lay out any Land that m^r hopkins hes Relinqushed
tiill further order
   Voted to adjorn this meeting to ye first Tuse Day
of September next at ten In ye morning.
       a True Record of ye above votes
                      Test Thomas Clark Clerk.

The proprietors Met according to adjornment on y^e
first Tuesday of September 1756 the meeting being thin
& no business appearing after ye meet was opened.
Voted to Adjorn this meeting to ye first Tuesday of
December Next at ten of ye Clock In ye fore Noon at
ye meeting hous
   A True Record of ye vots Test Thomas Clark Clerk.

The proprietors Met according to Adjornment on
ye firs Tuesday of December 1756
   At ye Same Meeting voted that ye Land Lately In
the ocupacy of John Southmayd Esqr of Waterbury
Deceas^d Commonly Called ye Little pasture. Shall be
for ye use of ye Severael Schools In ye Town of Waterbury to be Disposed of as as ye other School Lands here
to fore hath ben
   At ye Same meeting appoynted Dea^n Thomas Clark
& Ashbel porter to adjust a Mistak made In m^r
Stephen Hopkins farm In Respect of Land that was
took In belonging to ye proprietors

voted to ajorn this meeting to ye first Tuesday of March Next at 9 of ye Clock fore noon

    A True Record Test Tho: Clark Clerk

At A proprietors meeting Met according to adjorn-ment on March 1th 1757

ye meeting not being full Did by vote adjorn this meeting to ye 15 Day of this Instant at 9 of ye Clock In ye morning to Consider about Remeasuring our Lands & also of Disposing of ye village Land.

A True Record of ye vots Test Thomas Clark Clerk

At the meeting that met according to adjournment on ye first Tuesday of February A D 1756 at ye Same Meeting it was voted that ye Survey and plan of m^r Stephen Hopkins Farm In ye South East quarter of ye bounds In waterbury taken & made by Tho: Clark measurer with ye assistance of Capt Daniel Southmayd be alowd by this meeting and put upon Record and that he & his Heirs Shall for Ever possess and Enjoy all ye Lands Lying within ye S^d Generael plan which be fore this time Did belong to ye proprietors voted in the afirmative

    a true Record Test Thomas Clark Clerk

At a Meeting of ye proprietors Met according to adjornment March 15 1757 Whereas the proprietors voted In ye year 1731 that John Stanly Jun his Right to a Bachelder Lot Should be Good this meeting agree that ye Sd Jno Stanly Junr Shall be aded to the List of proprietors and have Right to Lay out his Divisions upon Sd Right from ye year 1730 and In all future Divisions

At ye Same Meeting Mesu^rs George Nicholes Josiah Brounson & Thomas Clark were Chosen a Committee

to Remeasur Doc^t Benjamins Land In Case he Calls
them to Do Sd work on his own Cost
Voted to adjorn the Meeting to ye Last Tuesday
of october Next at Nine of ye Clock In ye Morning
A True Coppy of ye Votes Test. Thos Clark Clerk

The meeting Met according to adjornment october
25.—1757 being a thin Meeting and no business pro-
posed voted to Adjorn this meeting to ye 3^d Tues Day
of December next at 10 of ye Clock In ye fore Noon

The Meeting Met according to Adjornment on y^e
3d Tuse Day of Decem^r 1757
At ye Same meeting at ye Request of Thomas Clark
for A Committee to Search his Records on ye account
of his Land being Lap^t at malmalick Capt Sam^{ll} Hikcox
& Capt Thomas porter was Chosen for Sd Committee
with full power to Give order to ye measurers to Lay
out according as they Shall find
at ye Same Meeting it was Voted that Capt William
Judd Shall Lay out a Lot In ye East Tear of Sixteen
acres & half to John Stanly Junr Joyning to ye Last
Lot
At ye Same Meeting Voted to adjorn this Meeting
to ye Next Tuesday at Eight of ye Clock In ye morning—

The proprietors Met according to Adjornment on
Tuesday ye 27 Day of Decem^r 1757 At ye Same Meet-
ing there was Chosen a Committee to Adjust matters
between ye proprietors & m^r Stephen Hopkins
Respecting a Quit Claim of his Land Lying above his
Land which Lyes within his plan and to order Sd
Quit Claim to be Recorded

At ye Same Meeting voted that their Shall be
a Division of our undivided Land In Sd Waterbury

at ye Same meeting voted to have a Division In
ye Sequester

At ye Same meeting it was Voted that there Shall
be Division In ye undivided Land of half an acre on
the pound to be Laid In Two Divison the first Lot
to be Drawn of one Quarter of an acre upon ye pound
and he that Shall Draw ye first Lot In yc first Divison
and So Successively ye Rest take ye Last In ye Last
Divison and So on

At ye Same Meeting It was Voted to part that peice
of Land Left at ye North End of ye Village & into
Said Divisons with ye following Regulations &
Restricktions viz Sd peice of Land to be Divided in
ye middle north and South and ye Laying out of Sd
Land Shall be in ye following manner & form begining at ye South End of ye East Tear Laying Lots
Joyning together & Runing through Each part East
& west and he that takes his Lot in ye Divison In
S^d Land Shall Relinquish five acres In his Divison for
one acre there

at ye Same Meeting Voted to have a Divison In
ye Sequter at ye Rate of five acres on ye Hundred In
ye propriety

At ye Same meeting Thomas Clark Esqr Capt Samuel Hikcox & Capt Thomas Porter appoynted a
Committee to prepare a Lot for ye proprietors for
next march

At ye Same Meeting Voted the Divison Shall begin
upon ye first Day of April Next Ensuing & Continue
Through April & may and then to Ceace till y^e
first of September Next and to Run three month and

So Successively Spring & fall till ye Divison is Run out very Stormy Days Excepted

The Meeting Adjorned to ye first Tuesday of March Next Ensuing

A true Record Test Thomas Clark Recorder

The order of ye Lott Drawn for on ye Divison Granted December 27. 1757 of half an acre on ye pound In ye undivided Land

1	School Lott	31	Richard Porter
2	obadiah Richard Se^r	32	John Richard Ju^r
3	John Barns	33	John Worner 4th proprie-
4	6th proprietor Lott		tors Lott
5	John Stanly Ju^r	34	Stephen upson Ju^r
6	Israel Richardson	35	Benjamin barns Ju^r
7	John Worner Se^r bach	36	Ephraim Worner
8	George Wellton	37	Timothy Hopkins
9	Second proprietors Lott	38	Stephen Hopkins
10	5th proprietors Lott	39	Thomas Richason Ju^r
	moses Brons	40	Sam^{ll} Porter
11	Joseph Bronson	41	John Bronson of Isaac
12	Tho: Newel	42	John Newel
13	Benjamin Worner	43	John Hikcox
14	Thomas Wellton	44	Sam^{ll} Worner of Thos
15	Thomas Bronson	45	John Judd Ju^r
16	John Scovel Ju^r	46	Benjamin Barns Se^r
17	m^r Jeremiah peck	47	Abraham Andrus Ju^r
18	first proprietors Lot	48	3^d propriety Lott
19	William Judd	49	Timothy Stanly Bach
20	Thomas Handcox	50	Stephen Wellton
21	Cap Thomas Judd William	51	Thomas Judd Jones
22	Abraham Andrus Cooper	52	John Southmayd
23	Benjamin Worner Se^r	53	150 propriety
24	John Hopkins	54	Robbert Scott
25	obadiah Scott	55	Joseph Lewis
26	John Worner Se^r	56	Isaac Bronson Ju^r
27	Thomas Richard Se^r	57	Philip Judd
28	Benjamin Richards	58	Abraham Andruss Se^r
29	Joseph Gaylard Se^r	59	Daniel Worner
30	obadiah Richards Ju^r	60	Thomas Upson

13

61	John Carington	82	Sam^{ll} Hikcox Se^r
62	Sam^{ll} Scott	83	John Wellton Ju^r
63	Edmund Scott Se^r	84	William Hikcox
64	Daniel Porter son of Dan^{ll}	85	Edmund Scott Ju^r
65	Stephen Upson Se^r	86	Richard Wellton
66	Timothy Stanly orig	87	Isaac Bronson Se^r
67	John Gaylard	88	David Scott
68	Sam^{ll} Stanly	89	John Wellton Se^r
69	Ebenezer Richason	90	Thomas Barns
70	John Stanly Se^r	91	Thomas Worner
71	George Scott Se^r	92	Joseph Hikcox Ju^r
72	Daniel Porter Se^r	93	John Bronson Se^r
73	Ebenezer Bronson	94	Thomas Clark
74	Jonathan Scott Se^r	95	Jonathan Scott Ju^r
75	John Judd Se^r	96	Thomas Judd Ju^r Hall
76	John Scovell Se^r	97	John Richards Se^r
77	Joseph Gaylard Ju^r	98	Thomas Andruss
78	Ebenezer Hikcox	99	Nathaniel Richason
79	John Richason	100	Thomas Richason Se^r
80	Joseph Hikcox	101	Thomas Hikcox
81	George Scott Ju^r		

An account of ye Divison Granted In the Sequester In December 27. 1757. of five Acres on ye 100 pound

1	2 proprietor Lott	40	16	Benjⁿ Warner Se^r	40
2	Obadiah Richard Ju^r	40	17	Ebenezer Hikcok	40
3	John Warner Se^r	162	18	Jonathan Scott Se^r	90
4	Richard Wellton	40	19	John Stanly Ju^r	40
5	Sam^{ll} Warner of Thomas	40	20	Thomas Judd William	180
6	Daniel Porter Se^r	171	21	George Scott Ju^r	40
7	6 proprietor Lott	40	22	Sam^{ll} Stanly	40
8	John Gaylard	40	23	Robert Scott	40
9	Thomas Barns	40	24	Joseph Gaylard Ju^r	40
10	Thomas Richardson, Se^r	90	25	Thomas Andrus	40
			26	William Hikcox	40
11	John Newel	180	27	John Scovel Ju^r	40
12	John Stanly	180	28	Benjⁿ Richards	40
13	Edmund Scott Se^r	180	29	Thomas Newil	162
14	David Scott	40	30	Stephen Upson Se^r	90
15	Ebenezer Brounson	40	31	John Wellton Ju^r	40
			32	Thomas Warner Se^r	180

33	Obadiah Richards	144	67	Philip Judd	144
34	John Judd Jur	40	68	Thomas Clark	40
35	Timothy Stanly orige	180	69	150 propriety Lott	150
36	Thomas Judd hall	180	70	Thomas Wellton	40
37	Abraham Andrus Ser	144	71	Nathaniel Richason	40
38	John Scovell Ser	144	72	John Judd Ser	180
39	Thomas Judd Jones	180	73	George Wellton	40
40	John Richards Jur	40	74	Ephraim Warner	40
41	first propriety Lot	40	75	mr Jeremiah Peck	270
42	Israel Richason	40	76	Thomas Upson	40
43	Abraham Andrus Cooper	180	77	Thomas Hikcox	40
44	Thomas Hancox	40	78	4th propriety Lot J Wr	40
45	John Richards Ser	144	79	Benjn Warner	40
46	Stephen Wellton	40	80	5 proprietor Lot	40
47	Richard Porter	90	81	Ebenezer Richardson	40
48	Thomas Brownson	40	82	John Barns	40
49	William Judd Bachelder	40	83	Timothy Stanly Bachr	40
50	Isaac Brownson Ser	160	84	Timothy Hopkins	40
51	Jonathan Scott Jur	40	85	3 proprietor Lott	40
52	Isaac Brownson Jur	40	86	Joseph Hikcox Ser	108
53	Danll Porter Jur	40	87	School Lott	270
54	Benjn Barns Jur	40	88	Stephen Hopkins	40
55	Abraham Andrus Jur	40	89	John Brounson of Isaac	40
56	Joseph Bronson	40	90	Leut John Hopkins	180
57	Edmund Scott Jur	126	91	Samll Hikcox	180
58	John Richason	40	92	Stephen Upson Jur	40
59	John Southmayd	270	93	John Wellton Ser	144
60	John Warner Ser bach	40	94	John Hikcox	40
61	Benjn Barns Ser	180	95	John Carington	108
62	Thomas Richardson Jur	40	96	Obadiah Scott	40
63	Thomas Richards	40	97	Samll Scott	40
64	Danll Warner	108	98	Joseph Hikcox Ser	180
65	Samll Porter	40	99	Joseph Lewis	40
66	Joseph Gaylard Ser	144	100	Georg Scott Ser	40
			101	John Bronson Ser	144

the proprietors Met according to adjournment on
ye first Tuesday in March 1758

at ye Same Meeting the Lot agreed upon ye Last
meeting was Drawn with ye order of ye Lott as may
be seen over Leaf

At ye Same Meeting Voted that Capt. William Judd Shall have power to Lay out Land In ye Southwest Quarter of ye bounds When Called to it

At ye Same Meeting Capt Thomas porter was Chosen a Committee with ye Town Clerk to Search Records for men that have Lost y^r Notes

at the Same Meeting Voted to Adjorn this Meeting to ye 3^d Tuesday of october Next of Nine of ye Clock In ye Morning

the Meeting Met according to adjornment october 17th 1758 the meeting very thin and no business appearing ye meeting adjorned by Vote to ye first weadens Day of march Next at ten a Clock in ye fore noon at ye meeting hous

the Meeting Met according to Adjornment ye first Wedensday of March next 1759

at ye Request of m^r Sam^ll Hopkins of Sheffield for a Commitee to be Chosen to Serch after his land at Brunsons meadow to Endeavour to find out what Land he had their and to make Return to ye proprietors meeting

At ye Same Meeting mes^rs Sam^ll Hikcox Thomas Clark & Thomas porter was Chosen a Com-tee for ye purpas above Sd//at ye Same Meeting voted to adjorn the meeting to ye first Munday of April Next

A true Record Test Thomas Clark Clerk

voted to adjorn this meeting this meeting to first munday of April next

The Meeting Met according to adjornment on ye first Munday of Aprill 1759

and voted that ye Lots In ye Sequester Shall be

prepared to be Drawn on ye first Tuesday of Sep^t Next and Like wise to be Drawn on Said Day

At the Same Meeting made Choice of Thomas Clark Esqr Capt Sam^{ll} Hikcox & Capt Thomas porter for a Committee to prepare Sd Draught

At the Same Meeting Granted Liberty to the Heirs of Capt Timothy Hopkins Late of Waterbury Deceas^d to Lay out 25 acres of Land at a place Called Brunsons Boggy meadow on ye East Side of Long Hill that is Now in ye Lawfull possion of Sd Heirs In order to fill up and Compleat ye Survey of their Farm and that they Shall Lay it out on account of the Divison Granted to be Drawn in ye Sequestered Land So far as ye Divison of Said Heirs in ye Sequestered Land will Go and that ye proprietors Clerk Shall have Liberty to Give them a Note to Lay out their Said Sequesterd Land Immeaditatly and that the Remainder of Sd 25 acres which their Sequester Land will not Draw may be Laid out on account of their Divison in ye out Land already Granted and Drawn

voted to adjorn this meeting to ye first Tuesday of September next at nine of ye Clock in ye morning

The meting met according Adjornment on the first Tuse Day of Sept 1759

At the same meeting the Lot was Drawn according to ye vote on ye first munday of April A D 1759.

At ye same Meeting voted that the Town Clerk shall Reserve 62 Acers of the Division Granted In Decem^r 27 1757 meaning John Worners propriety and that he shall not Give out any Note to Lay out ye Same

Voted to Adjorn this Meeting to ye first Tuesday of November Next at nine of ye clock in ye morning the Meeting Met according to Adjournment ye second Tuesday of Novembr in 1759

by reason of the meeting being so thin voted to adjorn this meeting to the first Tuesday March next at nine of ye Clock in ye morning

The Meeting Mett according to Adjornment March 4th 1760

At the Same Meeting voteed to begin ye Divison In the Sequester on the first Day of october Next

At the Same Meeting voted that m^r Joseph Bronson & m^r Sam^{ll} Hikcox Ju^r be added to the former Commite to Remove Encroachments from proprietors Land In the North West Quarter of the bounds

At the Same Meeting Voted that In Case any Man Se cause to Remeasur his Land according to art Shall find his Land want measure he may have Liberty of Laying out the wantage and if he have too much he Shall fill it up with Divison Land and ye Severael Town meas^r are here by Impowred with the help of an Artist to make Such Surveys for thus Regulating Mens Land

At the Same Meeting voted that Capt Judd Shall be Released from the Service of Laying out Land with in the South west Quarter of the bounds

at the Same Meeting voted to adjorn this Meeting to the first munday of Novem^r next

The proprietors met according to Adjornment on the first munday of Novem^r A D 1760 and No Business brough on and ye meeting very thin It was voted to Adjorn this meeting to ye Last munday of march Next at one of ye Clock after noon

the proprietors met according to adjornment on y^e
Last munday of March A D 1761

at the Same Meeting voted to adjorn this Meeting
to the Last Tuesday of october Next at ten of ye Clock
in the fore Noon

Grants of Land as Recorded in the
"First Book of Town Meetings"

Grants of Land

"Ye transcripts of land out of yᵉ old book into this began in febeary 1699 or 700."

[Att a meeting] in waterbury of yᵉ town: [there] was granted to John Judd four acers of upland northward from ye town aganst Left Standlys Common fenc provided he live here four yeirs and do not pregedis foremer grants[1]

Att yᵉ same meeting there was granted to john judd and john Richason [each] of them twenty acers of land on Steels brook on ye north branch [of] upland and swamp provided they live here four yeirs and do not pregde highways

[   ] 3 febeur 99: 700
[Att ye] same meeting there was granted to srg samll hikcox eyght acers of swamp and upland on yᵉ brook above Langtons timber provided he do not pregedis former grants highwayes nor dirifts of Cattell nor fetching [off] wood till it be fenct:

[Att a] meetteing of yᵉ propriators there was granted to srg samˡˡ hikcox thre acers [of land] on yᵉ east sd yᵉ Rivr aganst daniell Porters land at pine eyland not peregeding highways

[Att a] town meeting in watorbury genur 3: 1686 yᵉ town granted to srg samˡˡ [hikcox] four acers up yᵉ litle

---

[1] These grants are copied in the order in which they appear on the Town-book.

broock on ye north sd ye great lot to run from [hill] to
hill not to pregedis highwayes

[att a] town meeting decembr: 30: 1687 there was
granted to samuell hikcox [   ] of land on y^e
hill sid aganst his eyght acer lot:

[att a] town meeting in watorbury january 3: 1686
ye town granted samuell [hikcox] a couple of spongs
of bogey meadow on ye south sd of his addition already
layd out an acer or thre Roods

[att] a town meeting in mattatock decem 29th 1682:
there was granted to sam^{ll} hikcox an addition to his
alotment so much [up] land as shall make up his lot
to be an hundred pound alotment and this addition to
be aded to his eyght acer devition ye Com̄ ti: granting
ye same:

Att a town meeting in matatuck decembr ye 30:
1684 ye town granted to samuell scott half ye alotment
formerly granted to thomas Judd jnur with y^t exseption
of four acers to be taken out of y^t alotment [for a]
great lot —— and a divition of meadow with ye Rest of
ye propriators in y^e [   ] devition of meadow land
according to a fifty pound a lot with ye house lot on
ye south s^d of stephen ubson with theis provisals y^t
he build a hous according to articles within four yeirs
and live here four yeirs after his hous be built and pay
ye purchis of a fifty pound lot:

att a town meeting in mattatock decem 31 1684 y^e
town granted an addition to ye alotment granted to
samuell scott a three acer lot neer ye town as an addition to ye hous lot and eight acers after ye eyght acer
lots granted by ye Commity to y^e in habitants are layd
out provided his eyght acers be not taken up in y^e

town ship sequestered by y[e] town: nor pregedis former
grants

at a town meeting in mattatock decemb 31 1685: y[e]
town granted to samuell scott four acers of land in a
velly of lo land north ward of Judds meadow west sid
of y[e] River provided it do not hindr a highway nor
pregedis high ways

att a town meeting in watorbury decembr: 30[d] 1687
there was granted [to] samuell scott six acers of upland
joyning to y[e] part of his Eyght [acer lot]

att a meeting of y[e] propriators in watorbury decem:
22: 1690 there was granted to Jonathan scott teen
acers Joyning to samuell hikcox betwein wostor swamp
and bucks meadow on Conditions he settell in y[e] town:

att a town meeting i watorbury may 21 1688 Samuell
scott and Richard porter had liberty of Recording
lands formerly granted to them notwithstand[ing]
former ordor to y[e] Contrary

at a town meeting in watorbury genuary 3[d] 86: y[e]
town granted sam[ll] scott four acers in y[e] wigwam
swamp to run from daniell portor lot [eastward]

Trans scribed out of y[e] old book by me

Thomas Judd town clarck

trans scribd febe 99 700

att a meeting in watorbury of y[e] town ther was
granted to david scott five acers in y[e] swamp on y[e]
southwest s[d] of y[e] old town plat provided he live here
four yeirs and hinder not thos y[t] have [land] to make
use of or Com to y[e] brook for water

att ye same meeting was granted to david scott teen
acers of land up aganst bucks meadow north from y[e]
land granted to sam[ll] hikcox jun[r]

att a town meeting in watorbury there was granted

to John Richards and david [scott] eyght acers of
bogey meadow and upland at ye east sd of ye great
brook provided [they] improve it and coinhabit in y^e
town four yeirs after improvment not [to] pregedis
high wayes nor drifts of cattell

att a town meeteing in mattatock decem: 30: 1685
ye town granted to Edman scott all ye land betwein
ye Common fenc and east sid his own three acer lot
not to exstend furder southword then ye end of sd lot:

att a town meeting in watorbury decm: 30: 86 y^e
town granted to edman scott sianor five acers in y^e
west bogey meadow by thomas Richason at ye old
town plat.   if it do not pregedis former grants to but on
ye hous lots and Run throw ye meadow

att a town meeting in watorbury january 3: 1686 ther
was granted to edman scott senor a stripe of land on y^e
west sd ye River aganst his three acer lot so as to
Run his fenc on ye top of ye hill and but on john worner:

att y^t same meetting there was granted to edman
scott senor four acers on ye east sd of his soon samlls
lot at wigwam swamp

att a town meeting in watorbury decem 30 1687 y^e
town granted to edman Sott an addition to his four
acers lot to advance ye east Coner Stack teen Rods
southword and so to have ye land ajoyning

att a meeting in watorbury of ye town
there was granted to joseph gaylard senor five acers
of land on ye long hill on ye north sd ye path y^t leads
to john brunsons meadow buting on ye Rockey land
north and towards ye East sd of ye hill

att a town meeting in mattatock decmb 31: 1685
ye town granted to Joseph gaylard too acers of bogey
meadow at ye south end of his eyght acer lot upon y^e

acount of a Coner of his hous lot y^t he hath consented
to be layd out to ye high way by a commity apointed
by ye town

att a town meeting in watorbury gen 3: 1686: y^e
town granted joseph gaylard senor four acers of land
on ye north sd his too acers lying at ye heather end y^e
pople grinlet to join to y^t and run northward till he
hath his compliment. not pregedising high ways nor
former grants

att a town meeting decmbr: 30: 1687 there was
granted to joseph gaylard four acers betwein Robard
portors lot and his own at juds meadows in ye lo land
up among ye hills in a kind of a popple swamp

ye date torn of
att ye same meeting was granted to Richard portor
too or three acers of land upon ye hill aganst wornut
tree meadow buting on ye land belonging to ye great lot

att ye same meeting ye town granted Richard portor liberty to take his four [acer] lott on ye east sd of
john weltons and isaac brunson on ye burnt hill he not
hindrig them coming to theyr lots and relinquishing
his four acer lot up hancox brook nor pregedis hig ways

att a town meeting in watorbury decm 30: 1697: y^e
town granted to Richard portor four accres of land a
bove ye old fence up hancox brook—this 4 acres Removed by liberty & at liberty

att a town meeting in watorbury genua 29 1687 y^e
town granted Richard portor eyght acres joyning to
his brother daniells eyght acer lot

att a town meeting in watorbury aprill 17: 1688 there
was granted to Richard porter one acer and a half at y^e
loer end of his brother daniells land at ye pine eyland
also apeac at ye uper end of daniells land and so to

extend north ward to ye turnig of ye River not pregedising highwayes nor former grants

att a town meeting in watorbury decem 30: 1697:
ye town by way of acchang gave Richard portor y^e
highway betwein his hous lot and ye common fenc
for a parsil of land at ye east end of his hous lot to be
stacked out according as it was vewed by srg brunson
and abraham andrus senor ye high way next sd andruss
to be left 3 Rods wid and ye sd portor is not to hinder
them Coming to ye spring if ye sd loyn dont reach it
and sd portor is not to hinder men coming to mend
theyr com mon fenc

viz att a meeting in watorbury of ye town there was
12   granted to John scovell three acers of land at y^e
99   north east end of his bogey meadow Runing to
700   wood bury Roads

viz att a meeting of ye town in watorbury ther was
12   granted to Ephriam worner five acers of land on y^e
99   north end of ye Chesnut hill y^t buts on wood bury
700   path provided he live here four yeirs

att a meeting of y^e propriators in waterbury decem
22 1690 there was granted to Ephriam worner seven
or eyght acers of bogey meadow and upland abought
half a mile nor east at y^e wigwam swamp provided he
live here four yeer and build according to articles

october y^e 29 = 1707 layd out to obadiah Richord ju^r
deceased four acers and three Roods of upland at
Richards mountain butting every way on Common
land as part of his bachelder accomidations being under
improvement by plowing and three acers of bogey meadow upon woster swamp brook Commonly called

obadiahs meadow butting south westerly on ye up
land on a Rock and to extend northeasterly on each
sd ye brook by Timothy stanly measurer

aprill 14th 1708 a true Record of what was given
under ye measurers hand

Test. Thos Judd Register

trans	att a town meeting in watorbury there was granted
Cribd	to edman scott four acers of land on ye west
feb	and south sid of his four acer lot up ye great brook
99	he not pregedising high ways nor Coming to y^e
700	bogey meadows

at a town meeting in watorbury genuary 3–86 y^r
town granted edman scott jun^r four acers ye north end
to begin at Chesnut hill path and to Run from hill
to hill

att a meeting of ye propriators there granted to
abraham andruss jun^r and Edman scott the remainder
of ye land att juds meadow betwein edman scotts
eight acer lot and ye end of theyr meadow lots and
ye land granted to smith for a barn plat

att a town meeting in watorbury decembr 30 1687
there was granted to Robard porter one acer and a
half of land at ye norwest coner of his lot at ye flagey
swamp so as to reach ye spring

at ye same meeting there was granted to obadiah
Richards one acer of land on ye west end of his four
acer lot he not pregedising high ways

att a town meeting in mattatock decem 31 : 1685 y^e
town granted obadiah Richards one acer of land at
bucks meadow at ye south west coner of his own lot
to Run over ye broock to take ye leavell land on booth
sids ye broock

14

att a town meeting in waterbury genuary 29 1687
yᵉ town granted: obadiah Richards an adition of six
acers in yᵉ next divition of meadow provided he coinhabit five yeirs in yᵉ town from yᵉ date hereof

at a town meeting genuary 3 1686 there was granted
to obadiah Richards four acers up yᵉ little broock on
yᵉ north sd samˡˡ hikcox 4 acer lot

att a town meeting in watorbury january 3: 1686 yᵉ
town granted obadiah Richards a peice of lo land by
estimation an acer and hal or too acers on yᵉ west
sd yᵉ River south ward from stephen upsons eyland
a bove hancox meadow

att a town meetting in watorbury there was granted
to thomas Judd yᵉ smith leave to Rang with obadiah
Richards at yᵉ corner next to him not hindering high
wayes at litell brook

att a town meeting in watorbury yᵉ 3ᵈ of gnuary 86
there was granted to thomas Judd yᵉ Smith four
acers at yᵉ north end at his eyght acer lot

transcribd— ⌐ at a meeting of yᵉ propriators in
febewry: 99: 700 ⌐watorbury there was granted to
thomas Judd Smith three or four acers of land on yᵉ
hill aganst his lot at juds meadows not pregedising high
ways or former grants

att a town meeting in mattatock februry 25: 1695
the town granted to thomas judd soon of willyam Judd
yᵉ a lot ment formerly granted to yᵉ above sd willyam
Judd provided he com and inhabit four yers in a setled
or steady way from yᵉ first of may next ensueing with
yᵉ six acers granted for a pastor excepted

att a town meeting in mattatock december 31 1685
yᵉ town granted to thomas Judd yᵉ smith on yᵉ north
sd his hous lot to bute on john scovells three acer lot

to Run a parelel loyn with his till it com to butt on his own three acer lot

att a town meeting in watorbury march: 27: 1696 ye town gave liberty to deac judd for ye enlarging of his shop to make use of six foots of ye highway at ye east end of his shop so long as he improve it for y^t end

att ye same meeting was granted to thomas Judd juer four acers of land at ye north sd his four acer lot if it be ther to be had he not pregedesing high wayes

a town meeting in watorbury ye 3^d of genuary 86 there was granted to thomas Judd jun^r four acers of land on ye south end of ye great hill above John Wornors three acer lot aganst srg standlys fenc

febe 99: 700 transcribd

att ye same meeting there was granted to abraham andrus jun^r teen acers of land joyning to his eyght acer lot at ye bever ponds he not to pregedis highways

at ye same meeting stephen ubson had his given. joyning to timothy standly at derby bouns Abraham andrus had seven acers granted on ye sd hill

att a meeting of ye town janury 3^d 86 in watorbury there was granted to abraham andruss juner 3 or four accers joyning to his 3 acer lot at ye north and south east.

att a town meeting in watorbury there was granted to abraham andruss sener to spring out at ye north coner of his eyght acer lot so fare as to take too acers he not pregedising former grants

att a meeting of ye propriators in watorbury genuerry 22 1690: there was given to abraham andrus senor a peic of land buting on ye mill River and on ye common fenc aganst sd andruss three acer lot provided

it do not pregedis high wayes and he build a hous or
Set up a tan yard

att a meeting of yᵉ propriators in waterbury there
was granted to abraham andruss senr and to yᵉ heirs
of philip judd: deceased teen acers of land on yᵉ west
sd on theyr uper devition up yᵉ River five acers to sd
andrus and five to them

att a town meeting in watorbury january 3: 1686 yᵉ
town granted to abraham andruss snor five acers for a
paustor upon yᵉ little brook begining where yᵉ way
shall be layd out to begin at yᵉ north end of yᵉ playn
above yᵉ flagey swamp and so to run across yᵉ swamp
to yᵉ foot of yᵉ hill at yᵉ east sd and if he goes a way
within four yeirs it shall return to yᵉ town again

at yᵉ same meeting there was granted to samuell
hikcox juner three acers of land at yᵉ pine swamp
by yᵉ path yᵗ leads to yᵉ saw mill buting on yᵉ brink
of yᵉ hill takeing in all yᵉ swamp not pregedising high
wayes nor pasages   transcribed febury 99 or 700

att yᵉ same meeting there was granted to samll hikcox
juner four acers for apastor buting south on John brunsons three acer lot provided it do not pregedis high
wayes nor former grants

att a meeting of yᵉ propriators of watorbury genuery
22 1690: there was granted to samll hikcox juner
twenty acers of up land and swamp and and liberty
of takeing it up in too places a bought three quarters
of a mile east ward at woster swamp provided he live
here four yeirs and build according to articles

and five acers of bogey meadow at Cheesnut hill at
yᵉ north end of yᵉ long hill and west sd of Cheesnut hill
—and a peic of land aganst juds meadows buting west
on yᵉ River east on yᵉ hill and south on benjoanes land

more three aceres east from y^t up ye hill Runing
Cros our Road y^t leads to new haven on ye same
conditions of y^t above mentioned not pregedising high
ways

transcribd febew: 99 or 700   at a town meeting there
was granted to John Richason Willyam hikcox and
Joseph gaylard jun^r thirty acers of land att ye east
end of abragadow provided they improve it and in
habit four yeirs aftor improvement and build according
to origanall articles not pregedising high ways former
grants nor drifts of Cattell

att ye same meeting ye town granted to joseph
gaylard thomas hikcox john worner and thomas Richason four acers of land apeic in ye meadow y^t is called
by ye name of wolf pit meadow begining at ye south
end of ye meadow so Runing north word meadow
and swamp till they have got theyr 16 acers provided
they do not pregedis former grants high ways nor
drifts of cattell provided they improve it and coinhabit
four yeirs aftor improvement and perform origanal
articles:

transcribd febeury: 99 or 700   att a town meeting in
watorbury there was granted to John brunson four
acers of land up on ye great brook buting on gorg scott
north ye brook east ye high way west Runing south till
he has got his measure on ye same conditions gorg
scotts was given

att ye same meeting there was granted to thomas
hikcox and john brunson eyght acers upon ye playn
buting on ye north west sid of davids broock provided
it do not pregedis highways nor former grants and
improve and in habit according to former grants

att a town meeting in waterbury desembr: 30: 1686 there was granted to John Brunson apece of land at ye east end of his three acer lot to Rise upon a tryangle upon ye south as fare as ben barns provided he do not pregedis former grants nor high wayes

att a town meeting in waterbury   there was granted to m^r jeremiah peck and his soon jeremiah fifteen acers of land on ye southeast Coner of turcy hill he not pregedising former grants

att a town meeting in waterbury decem: 17: 1695: ye town Released jeremiah peck jun^r from his obligation of building on his hous lot lying by y^t which was formerly ben joaneses hous lot on y^t Conditions y^t he acsept m^r pecks three acer lot lying by ye mill river as a hous lot fullfill ye conditions of a hous lot and ye tarms of building according to original articles

att a town meeting in watorbury may 17 1694 ye town granted m^r peck should have y^t 3 acer lot joyning to y^t which belongs to john carritons heirs provided if it appear y^t there was any other three acer lot appointed to him he relinquish it

transcribd febeuy: 99 or 700

at a town meeting there was granted to gorg scott four acers of land up ye great broock buting upon edman scotts land north on ye great broock east ye high way west and to Run south till he has his four acers provided he improve it and inhabit four yeirs in ye town after improvement:

att a town meeting in watorbury: jun: 10: 1687 there was granted to gorg scott a peac of land on Steels playn buting on ye highway west on abraham andruss sen^r

north john worner and isaac brunson east and daniell
portor south provided he live here four yeirs

att a town meeting decembr: 30ᵈ: 1687 there was
granted to gorg scott four acers for a hous lot to run
southerly upon yᵉ highway yᵗ goes over yᵉ litle broock
at yᵉ north east Coner of yᵉ town to bute easterly on
yᵉ brow of yᵉ hill and so to Run westerly over yᵉ
broock and to bute northerly on the highway provided
he build a hous and live four yeirs in yᵉ town:

at a town meeting decembr: 30: 1687: there was
granted to gorg scott six acers of bogey meadow or
moving land abuting on yᵉ north branch of hop broock
where yᵉ broocks meet and to Run up yᵉ south
branch

att a town meeting in waterbury: aprill: 17: 1688
yᵉ town granted gorg scott six acers of upland on yᵉ
south sid of his six acers of meadow up hop broock not
to pregedis former grants

att a town meeting in waterbury may 20 1689 yᵉ
town granted mʳ peck and edman scott junʳ an addition
to yᵉ north end of theyr hous lots yᵗ is to say edman
Scott shall spring north words: 3 Rods on yᵉ north west
Corner and mʳ peck to spring a rod and half from yᵉ
northeast Coner of his lot and so a streyght loyn from
yᵉ above sd Corners to bound them on yᵉ highway
provided they make and maintain a good soficiant
ditch to dreane yᵉ land

att a town meeting in mattatock march yᵉ last 1685:
6 yᵉ town by voat determined yᵗ thos men yᵗ have
fenc over hancox broock northword from yᵉ town be
brought over to yᵉ east sd yᵉ broock and set in yᵉ rang
on as good ground as they now stand for fencing yᵗ

is in ye Rang y^t is detrmined furder to fenc for ye securing of ye meadows

at ye same meeting srg thomas judd and obadiah Richards and timothy standly was Chosen to lay out to thos men y^t remove over to ye east sd of hancox broock aganst joseph hikcox lot theyr proportions of fenc

at ye same meeting serg thomas Judd obadiah richards and timothy standly was Chosen to divid according to alotment to draw lots and lay out ye fenc forementioned

at a town meeting in waterbury genew: 3^d 86 ye Town by voate granted y^t all ye bogey meadows east from y town fenc too miles north and south word from ye town shall be sequestered for common lands and too miles east from ye afore sd fenc

att ye same meeting it is agreed by voate that in all theis lotsments there shall be liberty for any man to take wood ston timber or bushes in any of theis lots granted for pastor this day as long as they be unfenct and they are not to pregedis highwayes nor former grants

att a town meeting in waterbury march: 11^d: 1695 town agreed to Chang ye fenc belonging to ye scool land with stephen ubson Rod for Rod y^t is ye fenc belonging to ye scooll north from ye east gate

att a town meeting gna: 3^d 86 srg thomas Judd was chosen town measurer

att a town meeting jun 4^d: 96 tho judd jun^r was Chosen recorder for ye town

att a town meeting in mattatock decem: 30: 1684
the town determined that there should be a divition
of all ye undevided meadow to each propriator according to his meadow alotment former grants exsepted

att a town meeting in mattatock dec 31 1684 ye town
mad choys of srg Judd sam^{ll} hikcox and John standly
a commity to vew and prepare al ye undevided meadow
foralotmnt

att ye same meeting it was determinid y^t each man
should bare ye charg of laying out his 8^a lot

att a town meeting in mattatock march: 8: 1685; srg
thom Judd and srg Jn standly ware chosen patantees
to take out a patten for ye town ship:

att a town meeting in genurry: 3^d: 1686 ye town
declare ye worck of ye commity Chosen decm: 30^d
1694 namely srg judd sr standly & sam^{ll} hikcox was
to vew and prepare all ye undevided meadow up y^e
great River and up steels brook and hancox brook and
all ye branches up ye River

att ye sam meeting gen: 3: 86 ye town determined
y^t all ye land on ye east sid ye fenc Round to ye mill
River so to ye east mountain we say to davids broock
and to ye east mountain all ye land in y^t compas to be
and belong as common land or town plat

att a town meeting genuory 29: 1687 the town mad
choys of en sign Judd John wellton and samuell hikcox
to lay out what highwayes and pacages are need full a
bout ye town:

att a town meeting in waterbury march ye 2^d 1688
John Standly and timothy standly was appointed a
Commity to meet wallingford men ye 12 of this moneth
to agree of and state a loyn be twixt us

att a town meeting in watorbury march 27: 1696: y^e

town left the appointing ye time for burning a bought
ye common fenc to ye townsmen by beating ye drum
ye evening befor and so to attend ye same

att ye same meeting ye town consented to chang y^e
scool fenc y^t is aganst hancox meadow with thomas
Richason for his fenc at ye south end of thomas Judds
junrs fenc aganst steels meadow

att a town meeting may 17^d: 1694: ye town by
voate agree to use or improve ye money y^t now is or
here after shall be due for wild horses y^t are sould in
ye town we say to improve it for ye helping build y^e
meeting hous and to stand by ye oficers y^t sell them
and here after to a low thos yt bring in such horses
ye one half

att a town meeting in waterbury august 28: 1696:
where as ye law of fines y^t ye fenc vewers ware to go
by was by y^t law y^t was mad in may last to go by
Repayer ing ye fenc do chus to go by ye last law

att a town meeting in mattatock decembr: 26: 1682
John standly was Chosen Recorder for ye town

att a meeting of ye propriaters there was granted
to Stephen Upson three acers of land on ye west y^e
River on ye north sd wood bury Roade buting on y^e
brook y^t Coms out of ye bogey meadow

att ye same meeting left standly & ensign standlys
land was given by derby bounds.

there was granted to stephen ubson seven acers
joyning to timothy standlys lands

att a town meeting in mattatock may 7: 1686 ye town
granted to stephe ubson ye ground his barn stands on
and to Run a straight loyn to his gat porst

att a town meeting in watorbury genur: 3: 1686:
ye town granted stephe Ubson four acers of land for a

pastor on yᵉ north sd john hopkinses three acer lot
lying on yᵉ west sd yᵉ long hill

att a town meeting decem 30: 1687 yᵉ town granted
stephen Ubson four or five acers on yᵉ north sd his
four acer lot to spring to yᵉ hill at booth ends

att a town meeting in waterbury decm yᵉ 20ᵈ: 1697
yᵉ town acchanged yᵗ hous lot on yᵉ north sd of stephen
ubson with yᵉ sd ubson for too acers more or less as it
lyes formerly layd to sd ubson at yᵉ east end of his
hous lot

att a meeting of yᵉ propriators in waterbury there
was granted to Ensign thomas Judd three acers of land
on yᵉ South sd yᵉ Road yᵗ leads to farmingtown buting
on yᵉ high way and ye north Coner of his land lying
on yᵉ mill River

att a town meeting in watorbury decembr: 30: 1687
yᵉ town granted Ensign Judd an addition to his five
acer lot at yᵉ mad River from yᵉ mouth of yᵉ broock
to yᵉ fut of yᵉ hill north word and to take in yᵉ lo
land to Run an east loyn to a Rock from yᵉ foot of yᵉ
hill

att a town meeting in watorbury march: 27: 1696:
yᵉ town gave left Judd yᵉ high way on yᵉ west sd yᵉ
neck that Runs from yᵉ River to yᵉ hill on theis conditions yᵗ he leive as much on yᵉ north sd of yᵗ lot
yᵗ was joseph hikcox for high way

att a town meeting in watorbury january 3 1686 yᵉ
town granted srg judd five acers to begin at yᵉ mouth
of yᵉ broock yᵗ coms in to yᵉ mill River wher yᵉ mil-
stons were brought over

att a town meeting in watorbury febuary: 28: 169¾
yᵉ town granted Ensign judd liberty to advance at yᵉ
northend of his hous lots booth his own and yᵗ he

bought of daniell Wornor towards ye east coner of his
three acer lot he leiveing ye highway three rods wid

transcribed febeary 99 or 700   att a meeting of y^e
propiator they granted John Standly twelve acers lying
by derbe bounds on ye hill buting south upon ye devi-
dent loyn by derbe bounds on ye west sd ye River at
ye stacks set down by derby men.

att meeting of ye propriators of watorbury decembr:
22: 1690 there was granted to John Richards twelve
acers of land a bought three quarters of a mile up y^e
spruce broock a bove moun taylor on ye east sd y^e
great river on ye same Conditions sam^ll hikcoxs had
his of building and in habiting

att a town meeting in watorbury decembr: 3^d: 1686
ye town granted daniell portor four acers in ye wigwam
swamp as neare ye loer end as may be so as to have y^e
breath of ye swamp

att ye same meeting the town granted daniell portor
liberty to chang and take one acer by stephen ubson
upon ye playn aganst steels meadow for what he wants
of his eleven acers and grant him ye Remainder at y^e
west end of his lot at steels meadow

janury 6: 1696: att a town meeting ye town granted
doctor portor apece of land at ye south end of ye heyrs
of abraham andruses hous lot to run four rods south
and East with in twenty too foots of ye south east
east Conor of ye afore sd lot provided he build a tenantable hous with in three yeirs from ye date hereof

att a town meeting in mattatock decembr 29th 1682:
there was granted daniell portor by vertue of an agreement with him in reference to his lot by ye mill grant
him liberty of advancing south word from his stak at
ye south end of his hous lot as also in his three acer lot

upon ye west sd of sd lot advancing up ye hill makeing
a squor cornor next ye hill as ye hill Runs ye sd daniell
himself to bare ye damage y^t ye mill shall do to sd lot
provided also this grant is not to pregedis ye highways
    att ye same meeting thomas judd and john standly
was chosen to lay out daniell porters grant:

att a town meeting in watorbury decembr: 30: 1687
there was granted to John worner too acers of land
up ye first rising at juds meadows eastrly of daniell
portors lot:

att a town meeting decem: 30: 1687 there was
granted to isaac brunson one acer and a half at bucks •
meadow at his yard buting on ye yard—broock and to
Run south
    att a meeting of ye propriators in watorbury decm
22 1690 there was granted to isaac brunson juner teen
acers of land buting on ye bogey meadow at ye north
end of Cheesnut hill provided he live here four yeirs
aftor he is for him self

att a town meeting in waterbury ye 29 of a moneth
in ye yeir 1690 where as ye town having formerly
given Jeremiah peck ju^r ye one half of a great lot doe
now agree y^t he shall have y^t part belonging to y^t
lot lying in bever meadow as it was devided by Ensign
thomas Judd and srg sam^ll hikcox appointed for y^t
srvic Which is as follows—Wee whos names are under
Rited being desired and appointed by ye town to
divid a great lot in to too parts one part for jeremiah
peck and ye other part for ye scool have divided it as
follows
    Ĩ for y^e Ĩ part ye lot at ye loer end of ye bever

meadow betwein m͞r pecks and left standlys 2̄ three
Roods joyning to benjaman barnses lot in yᵉ neck as
it is now staked out 3̄ yᵉ uper sd of yᵗ lot in munhan
meadow as it is now staked out joyning to joseph
gaylards 4̄ yᵉ uper lot in hancox meadow 5̄ by four
acers lying on yᵉ east sd yᵉ Riveer aganst wanut tree
meadow

2̄ yᵉ scool part 1̄ yᵗ lot in yᵉ long meadow betwein
john brunson and Ensign Judd 2̄ three Roods in yᵉ
neck: as it lyes stacked out on yᵉ south sd of jeremiahs
yᵗ lys buting on ben barns 3̄ yᵉ south sd of yᵗ lot in
man han meadow buting southerly on yᵗ lot yᵗ was
john nuells 4̄ yᵉ great lot in hancox meadow lying
betwein john worner and daniell worner 5̄ yᵗ lot over
yᵉ Rivr aganst bucks meadow buting on obadiah
richards   devided by us this 4ᵈ of aprill 1690

Thomas Judd senor
Samuell hikcox senor

transcribed out of yᵉ old book by me

Thomas Judd town clark

yᵉ fenc all ready layd out belonging to jeremiah pecks
land above mentioned is as follows 1̄ fifteen Rods
on yᵉ south sd yᵉ south gate 2̄ yᵗ fifteen Rods yᵗ lys
nex john hopkinses fenc 3̄ teen Rods at yᵉ end
of abraham andruss senors fenc aganst yᵉ long
meadow

yᵉ fenc belonging to yᵉ scool land is 1̄ 21 Rods
at yᵉ south gate 2̄ fifteen Rods at yᵉ north end of
widow hikcox fenc up hancox broock 3̄ four Rods at yᵉ
north end of thomas wornors fenc in yᵉ last devition
north word from yᵉ town yᵉ dividing of this fenc
approved of by yᵉ town as it was divided by us

Abraham andrus
Thomas Judd   townsmen

The letting of ye Scool land
prise stated by a com-ty chosen by ye town
hancox medow 01—07—00 p^r yeir with ye 10 Rods of
fenc y^t was tho Richasons and 15 Rods at hikcox hools
y^t lot in ye neck six shilling with ye 3 Rods devition
y^e lot in munhan five shilling with y^e fenc at south
gate each of them to leive y^e fenc in good Repayer in
y^e judgm^t of y^e fencvewers but not oblidging them
y^t hire to make new
y^e lot att bucks meadow att 01—04—00 by y^e yeir
and to secure themselves.   y^e Com-ty
genuary 10th = 1705 y^e town ⎧ Tho-s Judd
by voate exsepted of this   ⎨ Richord portor
above ritten   ⎩ Joseph lewis
        Tho-s Judd clerk

an acoutt of land given and by lott to Tho mus Judd
the smith taken out of the propriters book: march
1710
    first a devition of ten acurs a man of upland granted
at a meeting of the propriters march 15 1691: taken up
at first at bucks hill and now by axchang with John
warner at the place cald Scots mountan ten acurs part
improvd:
    att a meeting of the propriters of water bury June
20 1692 thuer wus granted to John welton and Thomus
Judd the Smith to meet at John weltons fens on the
sd of the burnt hill
3)   at a proprieters meting held at water bury may
15 1699 theur was granted to deac Thomus Judd ten
acurs of up land wher he can find it one the sam condistions the young men have theirs not to pragodesh
hi ways nor former grants
    this land 5 acurs of it takcn up at a bogy madow

Southardly from buks hill the other at the uperend of woster swamp

at a meting of the propriters in waterbury fabru 22 1702/3 they gave liberty for decon Thomas Judd to relinquish his pich at the uper end of woster swamp and tak it at the west sid his land he had of John warner at scots mountan gining to his one land not to pragodish hi wais and former grants

4) att a meting of the propriteres in waterbury aprill 6: 1703 thear wus granted to deac Thomus Judd eaight acurs of land for a paster on the west sid of his land that wus John warners mountan

5) att a meeting of the propriters in waterbury jenywary 7th 1705 thuer was granted to deac thomus Judd six or seven acurs of land South of woodbury Rode be twen that and slead hall brook est from the west sid fens nt to pregedis hi wais formr grants

Tho Judd Recorder

att a town meeting at waterbury Jenuary: 29 1687 the town in order to ye makeing up of devition of meadow land in hancox meadow granted to severall men as follows   to thomas Judd ye smith one acer and a half joyning to his eyght acer lot   to ye heirs of joseph hikcox too acers joyning to ye part or remainder of theyr eyght acer lot that is to be taken up   to Ensign Judd three acers in ye valley on ye back sd of ye hill aganst hankox meadow betwein john worners lot and benjman barnses Common fenc   to thomas Judd juner one acer and a half joyning to his addition   to john worner too acers joyning to his grant of upland at juds meadows   to john Standly one acer on ye west sd ye River aganst hancox meadow aganst abraham andrus lot in part and ye coopers an tho Richason on ye east sd ye River to samll scott with his fathers consent too acers southwest from ye land layd out to him up bens meadow broock among ye hills   to philip judd one acer up on ye playn edman scotts and his own lot and joseph hikcox deceased and timothy standly lot att hancox meadow   to edman Scott juner on acer on ye south end of his four acer lot   to benjamin barns one acer and a half joyning to his four acer lot on ye east sd of ye long hill   to joseph gaylard one acer and a half at ye south end his bogey meadow   to abraham andruss senor too acer aded to his eyght acer lot   to daniell portor too acers aded to his eyght acer lot   mr (March) 2 <u>88</u> to benjamin joanes on acer and a half to be layd out to his eyght acer lot to make up his hancox meadow lot

att a town meeting in watorbury aprill: 17^d: 1688: upon ye Return of ye Commity in ye town Refering to y^t devition prepared by them to be layd out of meadow by ye agreement of ye town the town determined as followeth   first y^t Timothy standly Stephen Ubson and Samuell Scott should have theyr devition up hancox broock to pitch where they will not acSeeding three places and to have too acers for on instead of ye devition up ye River and wostors swamp—and daniell portor to have his devition where he can find it in any undevided land not voted or pitch upon by any former grants and giveing in to ye townsmen or Commity as they do up hancox broock and to have too acers for on ye sequestered land exsempted on ye east sd ye River   thomas worner to have too acers for on in ye devition of meadow at ye southword end of ye break neck hill as we go to woodbury and so to take up his whol devition   to John brunson was granted to

take his devition in ye same maner joyn to his bogey
meadow   to isaac brunson was granted his devition on
ye east sd ye Race playn buting north on ye high way
to woodbury to spring south and to have too acers for
one as others above said then and there by agreement

John wellton and edman Scott juner was to have y^e
meadow on ye west sid ye River containing by estimation 18 acers and too acers on ye east sd ye River
north word from it at ye north end ye bounds for
theyr devition: and ye men following for to take up
wostor swamp for theyr devitions Tho nuell Jn hopkins ben barns ben joanes Thomas Richason Joseph
gaylard Samll hikcox edman scott senor which land is
esteemed 46 acers to be devided according to theyr
proportion:

and Robard porter thomas judd jun^r and Richard
portor to have ye Remainder of jereco meadow on y^e
south sd Robard portors land Containing by estimation
4 acers and three Roods and seven acers at pine meadow and four acers adjoyning on ye north sd or west
of Ensign judds eyland to divid among them selves
according to theyr devitions — and m^r frayser and
smith judd obadiah Richards and daniell wornor to
have ye meadows up ye west branch: Containing by
estimation 29 acers to be devided as they agree

John Standly John worner john nuell john scovell
and john Carrinton are to take up pople meadow and
ye plains neare ye River on ye west sd ye River by it
and a meadow a bove it and twich gras meadow and
three Small meadows above it by estemation 30 acers
and devid it among them selves according to theyr
devitions of meadow and tho hancox and thomas
hancox to have a part of a lot ment with them

philip judd and abraham andrus senor to have

yᵉ meadow on yᵉ west sd yᵉ River neare yᵉ north end
of yᵉ bounds next john wellton Containing by eStimation 8 acers and a half and too acers and a half on yᵉ
east sd of yᵉ River in a small meadow aganst yᵉ loer
end of it by estimation eleven acers to devid it equally
according to theyr devition with yᵉ ReSt

att yᵉ same meeting aprill 17) 1688: Ensign Judd
was to have the meadow on yᵉ north of his eyland yᵉ
playn on yᵉ east sd of yᵉ River aganst it and one
acer up a playn above it on yᵉ north sid yᵉ River for
his own lot and his part of hancox meadow lot by
purchas too acers 3 Roods and eyght Rods and abraham andruss junʳ is to take his lot in yᵉ maner as
daniell portor and thomas worner have theyrs to take
it where he can find it with thos exseptions

april the 16 (1716 We hose names are Under riten
By order of the Propriators have laid out The sequestred Land according To the act that Is to Say two
mills East Bounded on a Chirsnet Tree marked with
TS and WᴴH With stons about it from Thence south
two mills with Trees marked to the south east Corner
which is a Chirs Net tree with a heap of stons about
it with marks—TS—WH from thence West to rock
with awhite oak—Marked with TS—WH and from
the east boundaries two mills north with trees marked
In the lien to the Corner awhite oake marked with—
TS—WH and from thence west To the Comon fenc to
a black oake tree east of the fence marked with—TS—
WH—   Timothy Standly
                                   William Hickox

aprill 23—1709 yᵉ measureing of yᵉ land in yᵗ field
yᵉ number of acers each man fences for and yᵉ pro-

portioning of y^e fenc Round sd feild With y^e number of Rods to each man on y^e east sd and West sd as it was stated and layd out by deac Judd Stephen Ubson and John scovell Com-ty for y^t end Chosen by y^e propriators of sd feild March = 14 = 1709 Layd to each acer in sd feild five Rods excepting a peic at y^e north end of y^e west sd left by y^e propriators to be dun in a generall Way:

Mr John Southmaid y^e east sd x north = east south = y^e West sd

	Rds	fo	in	foo	R	f	a	
M^r southmaid—	34	2 =	13 —	8$^{\underline{2}}$	5 =	6 = 10		R foot—
M^r south maid	Acers	R	feencd		east sd		West sd fenc	
	21—0—1		——		70—16 = 0		34—1—0	

y^e Record of y^e lot of y^e west sd fenc with y^e number of Rods as it fell and was lad out by y^e commity appointed march 14 = 1709 = beginning at y^e fals belo long medow

	Rods ft in		
serg brunson	6 = 3—9		
John Jud	48— 0—0		
Leiu^{tt} Tim Stanly	110—15—0		
Thos Richason	17—07—0		
Stephen Wellton	13—12—0		
Thos Richason	13—00—0 this out of portors		
Thos portor—	08—08—6		
abraham andrus	81—08—0		
Joseph hikcox—	23—03—0		
philip judd—	16—10—0		
personage—	47—12—0 out of this to m^r	R foot	
	southmaid	8—12	
sam^{ll} stanly—	57—11—0		
stephen hikcox—	27—15—0		
Thos nuell—	12—06—0 of this to serg	Rod foot	
	brunson	4—14	

	Rods ft in			
Thos judd ju[r]—	34—03—0	seg brunson out of	R	in
		Th judd and john	2— 8—6	
		judd out of ye		
		north end of the	Rod	
		judds fenc	8— 0—0	
obadiah Richards	09— 0—0			
Widow andruss—	29—09—0			
doct portor—	62—10—0			
Stephen Wellton	35—01—0			
edman scott—	59—13—0	doct portor out of	Rods	
		ye south end this	8	
gorg scott——	23—00—0			
M E bull—	24—12—0	Tho Richason out	Rod foot	
		of this	1—13	
John Wellton—	25—13—0	and out of this	Rod	
		Thos Richason	2—12	
Richard portor	42—07—0	jeremi peck out of		
		ye north end		
Wiliam hikcox—	03—02—0	ben berns out of	RD	
		portor	1—13	
benj barns—	54—01—0	widow joans of		
		portors	5—05	
jeremi peck—	35—04—0			
John hopkins	50—13—0			
Mill land—	80—06—0			
John Richords	62—03—0			
mr southmaid	02— 0—0			
jon judd——	19—04—0			
deac Th Judd—	138—00—0			
William hikcox	41—13—0			
John scovell	57—02—6			
John Richason	06—03—0			
mr south Maid	23—00—0			
Thos hikcox	31—01—0			
Stephen Ubson	74—00—0	jonathan scott out	Rod foot	
		of this	17—11	
John Wornor	02—00—0	jonth scott out of		
		yt was ebenez hik-	Rod foot	
		cox fence	3— 5	
		thos hikcox out of	Rods foot	
		ebener hikcox		
		fenc	7— 2	

now ye gaps being [s]toped as may be seen—how men
are layd at ye end their loyn We go to ye uper end y^e
north for them y^t want their proportion in this *devition*
(a line gone)
    ye first at ye north end and ye West sd fenc
John Wornor Which is now

	Rods foots		Rods foots
david scotts	24—11	samll stanly	30—04
John Judd	14—00	Stephen Wellton	21—07—6
Leiutt Tim Stanly	14—08—6	John Wellton Senr	22—05
John brunson	11—07—6	jeremiah peck	17—01
abraham andruss	05—00	Mill land	17—02
John Richason	14—00	John Richards	15—13
philip judd	03—03	John Carrington	03—06

in persuantt of an act of the propriters at a met in
march 5: 1711 we whos nams are under writen laid
outt to John Richards and william hickcox in fens at
the north end of the fens on the west sid in march
12th 1711

Rods

    to william hickox   25—00 ⎧ thomas Judd smith
    to John Richards   50—00 ⎨ John Richards
                                              ⎩ William hickox

an acount of the origanall grand propriters with their
number as they war setteled by the grand commyty
from 150 to 50 is as folows

m^r Jeremyah peck	150	John warner—	090
m^r John south maid—	150	Thomas warner—	100
Jeremyah peck and scooll—	150	John brumson sn^r—	
Left Timothy standly—	100	Isaac brumson—	
Left Thomus Judd—	100	William Judd—	100
Left John Standly	100	benjemen Jons—	100
John Welton—	100	Thomus Judd ju^r—	
edmun scott sn^r—	100	John Scovell sn^r	080
abraham andruss sn^r—	080	Thomus hand kox—	100
abraham andrus j^r—	100	John newill—	100

Thomas newill—
benjamin barns—
Joseph galerd—   100
John hopkins—   100
samll hickox—   100
Joseph hickox—
doc danll porter—
edman scot jur—   100
obadyah Richards—

philip Judd—
Roberd porter—
John carington—
stevn upson—
danill warner—
Thomas Richason—   050
Richard porter—   050
samll scott—   050

transcribd febeury 99 or 700

at ye same meeting of ye propriators there was
granted to timothy standly 12 acrs buting on ye fore
mentioned peic of land of John standlys buting on
derby bounds as conveniantly as may be

att a town meeting in watorbury genuary 3^d 1686
ye town granted timothy Standly four acers att the
south end of smith judds eyght acer lot on ye west sd
ye great River.

att a town meeting decem: 30: 1687 there was granted
to timothy standly six acers of bogey meadow up
toantick broock

att a town meeting there was granted to srg timothy
standly three acers northerly buting on his four acer
lot at standlys timber not pregedising high wayes

att a town meeting in watorbury decm: 30: 86 y^e
town granted eyght or teen acers of land on ye east
sd of ye branch of ye mad River on ye Right hand of
ye new Road as we go to fermingtown we say grant to
philip judd

at a town meeting genua 3: 1686 ye town granted
philip judd four acers on ye south sid of abraham
andrus sno^r lot up ye little broock

transcribd febeury 99: 700

ye propriators granted to john wellton senor teen acers up ye brook south word of joseph gaylords bogey meadow a bout a quarter of a mile from worenog hill

att a town meeting in waterbury genuary 29: 1687 the town granted to john wellton sener eyght acers to be aded to his next devition of meadow

att a meeting of ye propriaters in waterbury decm 22 1690 there was granted to john wellton junr twenty five acers of land west word from abraham andrus sen and y^t which was philip judds uper devition a bought half a mile from sd andruss and juds land provided he live here four yeirs and build a hous according to articles

att a town meeting in waterbury may: 21: 1688 ye town granted John wellton ye land a jasent to his too acer lot in ye little meadow on ye west sd ye River south word from ye town which he hath in improvement—and to Record it provided he do not pregedis high wayes.

att a town meeting in waterbury january 3 1686: there was granted to John Wellton twelve acers of land provided he do not take it within a mile of ye town or any bogey meadow or swamp nor pregedis highwayes or former grants

att a meeting of ye propriators there was granted to benjamin barns one acer and a half on ye west end of his five acer lot at juds meadow and a peic in ye mad meadow ye breadth of his lot to ye fenc:

att a town meeting decembr 30: 1687 there was granted to benjamin barns four acers of land a buting up on ye nor west coner of his lot at juds meadow to

run north word in a valey under ye hill on ye south
west sd ye broock

att a town meeting in waterbury january: 3: 1686
ye town granted benjamin barns four acers on ye east
sd ye long hill up on a grinlit y^t Runs into y^t broock
y^t runs in to ye broock Called carrintons broock

att a town meeting in waterbury decm 30 1686: the
town granted benjamin barns apece of land at ye east
end of his three acer lot provided it do not pregedis
ye high way

att a town meeting | may: 7: 1686 ye town granted
thomas worner one acer of land on ye west sd ye River
aganst ye mouth of ye Cove aganst ye neck:

att a town meeting in watorbury genuary: 3: 1686:
ye town granted thomas worner too acers of land up y^e
second brow east word of daniell portors land at juds
meadow

att a town meeting in watorbury genuary 3: 1686
there was granted to thomas worner four acers on y^e
Right hand on ye way y^t leads to farmingtown over
ye mill River to begin at ye bever pond broock and
so run northword

att a town meeting waterbury gen: 3: 1686 ye town
granted John Carrinton four acers on ye north sd y^e
mil river at ye mouth of ye broock calld carrintons
broock

att a town meeting at watorbury decembr: 30^d:
1687: ye town granted John hopkins y^t a lot ment
now in his posession which was formerly deac langtons
freely and absolutely to him and his heirs forever
exsepting y^t a lot ment in Isaacs meadow Containing

three acers and y^t too acer a lot ment in hancox meadow
which still abids intayld to ye mill as appears by y^e
town act febeur. 13: 1682: we say theis too lots are
intayld to ye mill as ye 30 acers was in tayled by y^e
Commity

att a town meeting in waterbury january 3^d 1686
ye town granted John hopkins four acers of up land
where he can find it provided it doe not pregedis highwayes or former grants

att ye same meeting jen 3: 86 ye town granted John
hopkins a peice of land at ye east end of his hous lot
provided it doe not pregedis highwayes

att a town meeting in waterbury decembr: 30: 1687
the town granted thomas Richason one acer on ye east
coner of his four acer lot provided it do not pregedis
highwayes

att a town meeting in waterbury jenuary 3^d: 1686
ye town granted thomas Richason four acers for a
pauster on ye north sd of joseph gaylards four acer
lot up popell grinlet

att a town meeting in waterbury may 17: 1694 y^e
town granted John Richards liberty to let his hous
stand where now it is and to have ye land and to Run
to ye Reare of john hopkinses hous lot he seting his
fence on ye south sd of ye path y^t now leads to y^e
corn mill and thomas judd ye smith was apointed to
stacke it out to him and john Richards is to Relinquish
y^t part of his lot y^t Runs ye north sd ye path y^t leads
to ye Corn mill

att a town meeting in waterbury: june: 5: 1696:
ye town ye town gave john Richards leave to Record

y^t lot under ye long hill joyning to ye bogey **meadow** given to sd Richards and david scott as it was **layd out** by ye town measurer

T. J Recordr—

Report of Committees on Mill Lands
1851.

Report of Committee on Mill Lands
1851.

The undersigned a Committee appointed at a meeting of the Proprietors of the Ancient Town of Waterbury on the 4th day of January 1851 to enquire into any lands heretofore granted by the State of Connecticut on Condition—Respectfully Report

That in the year 1679 a committee of the then Colony of the State of Connecticut recommended that a Corn Mill be built at Mattatuck & for encouragement granted thirty acres to such persons, their heirs & assigns forever as should erect a Mill there upon condition they maintaining said Mill forever—

That in Feby 1680 the same committee ordered that Stephen Hopkins who had built a mill at that place should have the thirty acres appointed in their former order—and so much more added to said thirty acres as would advance the same to be in value of 100 Pound allotment and also a house lot of two acres to suit the mill & appointed two persons to lay out said land—

And that afterwards at a town meeting in 1682 the town also granted to Stephen Hopkins Deacon Langton's allotment with the provision that one half of it should be entailed to the mill as the thirty acres had been—

That it appears from the Records that these thirty acres were afterwards laid out pursuant to the Grant of the Grand Committee & some other lands but it does not appear that said Mill which was then built, was upon s^d land so laid out—or that the mill was located in any particular place—

And we further find that from that date said lands have been regularly conveyed from one person to another down to the present occupants some by deeds of Quit Claim & some by Deeds of Warranty— without any reservations in the same & warranting against all claims whatsoever—& free from all conditions—and that in some of the Deeds of the Mill Lands as then called—the Mill & privilege is named as a separate part of the property & distinct from the same—

And we further find that from the long lapse of time and the course of conveyences of said property and the impossibility of now determining the precise location of the said lands—we recommend that the subject is not deserving of further attention and for the purpose of quieting all further agitation on the subject we recommend the appointment of a Committee of two in lieu of the one appointed at the last meeting to release to any of the present owners of said property or any other property any rights that the ancient proprietors may have to lands heretofore granted upon conditions as aforesaid

We also find that the grant of said lands was from the State of Connecticut instead of the Ancient proprietors & that if there is any reversionary interest as to said lands—the title is in the State of Connecticut instead of the Ancient proprietors of Waterbury.

Dated at Waterbury Jany 25th 1851.

Samuel H. Nettleton
Silas Hoadley
Josiah Hine

[In pencil:] Voted to accept the above report.

[The body of this is in the handwriting of Norton J. Buel. The pencil memerandum is by Cha⁵. D. Kingsbury, proprietors' clerk

F. J. Kingsbury.]

At an adjourned meeting of the Proprietors of the common & undivided lands of the Ancient Town of Waterbury legally warned & held at Gothic Hall in Waterbury on the 25th day of January 1851—The following vote was duly passed—
VOTED—That Willard Spencer and John P. Elton be and they are hereby appointed a committee for and in the name and behalf of the Proprietors of the common and undivided lands of the ancient Town of Waterbury to release and convey by proper Deeds of conveyance to the present owner or owners of any lands known as the Mill Lands and all others heretofore given or granted on conditions by a Committee appointed by the State of Connecticut or by any subsequent Committee or Committees of the Ancient Town of Waterbury, all the right title and interest that the said Proprietors may or ought to have thereto and also to release and discharge said lands from said conditions.
The foregoing is a true copy of Record.
Attest C. D. Kingsbury Proprietors Clerk.

TO ALL PEOPLE TO WHOM THESE PRESENTS SHALL COME—GREETINGS:

KNOW YE THAT WE The Proprietors of the Common and undivided Lands of the Ancient Town of Waterbury by Willard Spencer & John P. Elton our Committee thereto specially authorized and empowered by a vote of said Proprietors in legal meeting assembled, a copy of which vote duly certified is hereto annexed and made part of this deed, for the consideration of One Dollar received to our full satisfaction of The Scovill Manufacturing Company, a corporation located & established in the Town of Waterbury, in New Haven County, do remise, release and forever Quit-Claim unto the said Scovill Manufacturing Company their successors and assigns forever all the right, title, interest claim and demand whatsoever as we the said Releasors have or ought to have in or to a tract of land situated in the Town of Waterbury Easterly from the Public Green containing thirteen acres more or less Bounded Northerly on Highway, Heirs of Joseph Porter, Jesse Porter, Heirs of Eunice Baldwin, Scovill M. Buckingham, Daniel Porter, Julius and Wheeler Perry, John D. Johnson or land lately owned by him, Easterly on said Johnson or land lately owned by him and Thomas Kilduff, Southerly on said Kilduff, Prospect Road, Abner J. Leavenworth and Charles Reed and Westerly on Highway, with all the Buildings thereon standing, water privileges and fixtures thereon standing—Being the same premises deeded to said Releasees by J. M. L. and W. H. Scovill by their deed dated January 28th, 1850, on Waterbury Land Records, Vol. 54, Page 416—and we hereby release and discharge the above described premises from all the conditions that may have been imposed upon the same in the original grant thereof by the Proprietors.

To HAVE AND TO HOLD the premises, with all their appurtenances unto the said Releasee their successors and assigns forever, so that neither we, the Releasors, nor our successors nor heirs nor any other person under us or them shall hereafter have any claim, right or title, in or to the premises, or any part thereof, but therefrom we and they are by these presents forever barred and secluded.

IN WITNESS WHEREOF, we the said Willard Spencer and John P. Elton being thereto authorized and empowered as aforesaid for and in the name and behalf of said Proprietors have hereunto set our hands and seals this 28th day of January A.D. 1851.

Signed, sealed and delivered in presence of
A. M. Blakesley
David B. Hurd

Willard Spencer (L. S)
John P. Elton (L. S.) } Committee.

NEW HAVEN COUNTY, ss. Waterbury, January 28th, 1851.

Personally appeared Willard Spencer and John P. Elton signers and sealers of the foregoing instrument and acknowledge the same to be their free act and deed and the free act and deed of the Proprietors of the Common & undivided lands of the Ancient Town of Waterbury before me.

David B. Hurd, Justice of the Peace.

Recd. for Record January 29th, 1851.

& Recorded by Theodore S. Buel,
Town Clerk.

Vol. 57, pp. 115–116.

APPENDIX

I

To Timothy Stanly and Abraham Andrrus
 Selectmen of Mattatuck these:
Haveing received letter signed by yo^rselves Dated feb^ry: 20th, 1681, wee underwritten have returned in answer to yo^{rs} as followeth.

1. In referance to that Question which of the great Lotts shall be for the minister's use,

we leave it to yor Judgm^t to be determined by the Majo^r: part of the inhabitants, and if you cannot agree we shall determin,

2Q: in referance to the great Lotts our answer is, men at present to take up those Lotts do not appeare to us, we are not forward to break them, hoping in time some of worth and usefullness may appeare, and for the present leave it in the hands and power of Serg^{t.} Thomas Judd serg^t: Jno: Stanly and Samuel Hikock to let out the three great Lotts, and to break up Two or three acrs in each Lott, and to defray all common charges.

3Q: in reference unto a ways to be laid out for passag through yor meadow Lands, Our Answer, that we desire and appoint the fore s^d: sergt. Tho. Judd Serg^t: Jno: Stanly and Samuel Hikcox, to lay out ways through s^d: meadows of Twenty foots wide or more if they Judg needfull, for cart, Horse, and oxen in yoak every man to hould the propriety of the land that shall be taken out of his and their allotments, forever, only to be improved for the use a foer sayd of a passage, the pasterage to belong to him or them through whose lott the way shall be laid out,

Whereas we rec^d: a paper signed by Serg^t: Thomas Judd Isaac brunson, and Benjamin Jud in referance to herding of cattle,

we doe order and appoint for the future, that the inhabitants being orderly convented at a Town meeting, the Major part of the inhabitants so met shall have full power, to resolve and determin the way and method for herding of Cattle, and to state what shall be charged for keeping of Cowes, and what shall be levyed on dry Cattle.

signed by us

Jno Talcott
John wadsworth } Committee
Nicho Olmstead

Hartford Aprill 5th 1682.

II

THESE may Certifie all whome it doth or may Concern That I Thomas Kimberly surveyor of Lands in the County of Hartford on the 6th day of May, Anno Dom. 1715. At the Desire & in Company with Mr. John Hopkins, Danl Porter, and other men of the Town of Waterbury in Order to Survey and find the breadth from East to West of the Southern bounds of the Said Township of Waterbury, And I begann at two Chestnut trees markt, standing on the Westerly Side of a Run of Water, at Some distance Northerly of a boggy Meadow, which trees Stand at the South West Corner of the bounds of S^d. Township, and at South Easterly corner of the bounds of Woodberry. From Thence I ran East by the needle of the Instruement. 3. miles and 36 rods to the River Called Naugatuck, viz. the Westerly bank thereof, and from thence We ran South (by the Needle) one Mile & 20 rods (Crossing the Said River) to a brook running W. falling into the S^d. River in the Southern bounds of the Said Township of Waterbury next

Derby. from thence I proceeded on my former Course E. one Mile, then made another offset of 80 rods. Then again Continued our Course E. 1 miles and 120 rods, falling 10 rods N. of 3 Chestnut trees standing at the N. E. Corner of the Bounds of Milford and N. W. corner of the bounds of New Haven * * * Commonly called the 3. brothers, alias, three Sisters (as these Gent^{ln} informed me) Then Course continued—I ran E. one Mile, and fell 80 rods N. of a White Oak tree Markt anciently, and a large [heap] of stones about, and diverse Letters & figures on s^d tree Standing on the Southerly side of Wat. land. From that tree E. ran 13 Changes. wanting 16 rods to a heap of Stones (on the Top of a bare Mountain) by us now Erected for the E. bounds of the Said Township of Waterbury. A Map of this survey is hereunto annext. Here Note that a Line drawn E. from the first mentioned Chestnut trees till it Intersect a line drawn N. from the mentioned White Oak tree, in length is, 6 miles & 156 rods and that in this 6 mile & 156 rods no allowance was made for the roughnesse and unevennesse of the Land, whereas according to my best skill there ought to be allowed, at least, 118 rods.

Tho. Kimberly—Surveyor.

INDEX

The lists of names not indexed may be found on pages 69, 70, 77-79, 81, 99-100, 113-116, 123-126, 131-132, 136-140, 145-146, 155-158, 171-179, 193-195, 228-231.

249

Index

www.ingramcontent.com/pod-product-compliance
Lightning Source LLC
Chambersburg PA
CBHW070610270326
41926CB00013B/2487